Negotiate Anyw

Gavin Kennedy runs Negotiating Clinics and
Seminars in the UK, Scandinavia, Australia,
South Africa and the USA, together with the
co-authors of his highly successful first
negotiating book *Managing Negotiations,* now
in its second edition. He is also the author of
Everything is Negotiable! Gavin Kennedy is
an economist teaching in the Business School
at the University of Strathclyde. He is
married with five children and lives in
Edinburgh.

Negotiate Anywhere!

Gavin Kennedy

ARROW BOOKS

Arrow Books Limited
62-65 Chandos Place, London WC2N 4NW

An imprint of Century Hutchinson Limited

London Melbourne Sydney Auckland
Johannesburg and agencies throughout
the world

First published by Business Books Ltd 1985
Arrow edition 1987

Printed and bound in Great Britain by
Anchor Brendon Limited, Tiptree, Essex

ISBN 0 09 947120 5

For Karen

Contents

Preface

This book should be regarded as an extension of my previous book *Everything is Negotiable!* (1982). It follows the same format and much of the material in it has featured over the past few years in my international negotiating seminars.

The most common question I get from negotiators in any country is: 'How do you rate negotiators from other countries?' I find this a prelude to some of the most illuminating discussions we have at the Negotiators' Clinics, particularly when the participants are of mixed nationalities.

Negotiators, from the most experienced through to beginners, are always interested in each other's styles and whether this or that culture produces the 'best' or most 'natural' negotiators.

I have always insisted that there is no such thing as a 'born negotiator' and I am more than ready to assert that no one culture or nationality produces 'better' negotiators than another. I firmly believe that negotiating is a skill that can be learned and no matter what level of skill that anybody has at any moment they can improve their performance by training and experience.

Just as firmly, I believe that different cultures have produced different styles of negotiating, whether it is in the pace at which they conduct their business, or in the more common of the tactics they employ to secure their objectives. Add to this cultural background the unique economic and political features of a society and you have almost completely defined the content and method used in the negotiations in which they are involved.

This book can be seen as a summation and extension of the content of those seminars that have dealt with the importance of culture and background in the negotiating processes that the international business community finds necessary in order to conduct its wealth-creating foreign-trade.

Negotiate Anywhere! has no claims to being an exhaustive survey of every country and every culture in the world of business. I have been selective of some of the major trading areas in order to concentrate on important features that negotiators who want to do better must consider if they are to do so.

I look at negotiating styles in both capitalist and communist countries, in the Middle East, North America, Japan and Europe.

My central message is that you can negotiate abroad providing you remember that culture does influence your partner's behaviour and that if you want to do better in your negotiations you had better become aware of the influence your partner's culture is exerting on him or her and, as important, the extent to which you are influenced by your own culture.

I have met many hundreds of international negotiators over the past twelve years and many of them have influenced the contents of this book. To all of them I offer a totally inadequate but nevertheless sincere thanks for all they have taught me.

My co-authors of an earlier book, *Managing Negotiations* (1980), John Benson and John McMillan, have continued to exert their individual and unique talents upon my thinking about negotiating, and in numerous instances in this book their influence has been instrumental in what I have said (though they are absolved from any responsibility for the way I have inadequately done justice to their clear thinking).

My colleagues at the Strathclyde Business School have been indulgent in my favour when it has come to finding time for me to write the text; my family likewise have been their usual helpful selves while I have been fiddling about on the word processor.

The fact that the book has appeared at all is due to the support received from Vivien James at Business Books. That readers are the final arbiter of a book's merits has always guided my work and I therefore extend to all my usual invitation to write and tell me your views.

Gavin Kennedy
22 Braid Avenue
Edinburgh
EH10 6EE
Telex no. 72165

1 Dogs are different
or, why trade and wealth go together

The importance of trade

Trade or stay poor. That is the bottom line for every country that aspires to survival in the world economic system.

It doesn't matter whether you are exporting or importing, piling up raw materials, processing bits and pieces, assembling parts, packaging entire plants or selling on what others have sold to you, nor does it matter whether you are a capitalist or a communist (or anything in-between), a saint or a sinner, a Christian, a Muslim, a Hindu, a Confucian, a Jew, an atheist or a even a devotee of voodoo, and it certainly doesn't matter whether you are rich or poor, deserving a break or due a come-uppance: if you don't trade profitably you won't trade for long and if you don't trade at all you will have sealed your fate as surely as if you had gone in for free-fall parachuting – without a parachute.

There is just no way in which the goods and services that the rich countries take for granted can be got by those who can pay for them without the act of trading. And there is no way in which the goods and services that the poor countries quite rightly aspire to possess can be got on a long-term basis unless they trade for them.

Those societies that attempt to distribute their goods and services without trade must almost always compromise their no-trade principles or face a steady ruin of their people. What is not permitted by law breaks through illicitly: the people will trade whatever the risks, whatever the bureaucrats threaten to do to them, and whatever names they are called by the dictators. Those whom the dictators condemn as 'bandits', 'social parasites', and 'traitors' are actually regarded (rightly) by the people they serve and supply as heroes: they provide the people with the one thing the dictators usually keep for themselves, namely, *choice* of things to consume.

1

TRAGEDY AT MAKOLA

Ghana's economy has been going through a bad time and a recent collapse in economic confidence led to a military coup. The military had good intentions but remained economically illiterate. Faced with serious food shortages and rapidly rising prices they chose the age-old method of intervention.

This never works. They sought popularity by blaming the shortages on black-market stock-piling; they took stern measures against smuggling; they instituted price controls and finally they turned the mob on the market traders at Makola (Accra).

The mob destroyed the market by fire, violently dispersed the market 'mammies', and still went home hungry.

By intimidating the only people who could be mobilized to get food into Ghana – not by exhortation but by self-interest – the government perpetuated the shortages. If it had told the market mammies that they could keep all their profits from trade, if they had repealed all laws against smuggling, and if they had abandoned price controls – in other words the exact opposite of what they did – they would now be ruling a fitter, fatter and well fed Ghana.

Why? Because it is a law of human nature that if you make it worth somebody's while to put themselves out they will always do so, and if by doing so they bring in food to a starving country they will do more good for the people than any other grouping. Next door to Ghana, the Ivory Coast has none of Ghana's draconian laws about food prices. It is also suffering none of Ghana's self-inflicted ailments.

So-called 'black-market' traders are the very creation and, therefore, life-blood of any society that suppresses the freedom of trade. Destroy them and you immediately reduce living standards. Instead of being blamed they should be praised, instead of being pilloried they should be saluted.

Adam Smith

Way back in the 1770s, about the time when George Washington and his friends were stirring themselves to fight for the right to trade without English interference, a Scotsman, Adam Smith, had recognized the importance to civilized society of the act of trading and was working on it as the major theme of his *magnum opus, An Inquiry into The Nature and Causes of the Wealth of Nations* (1776).

Smith took twelve years to write his great work (much of it dictated to his sister while warming his rearquarters over his coal fire and drinking claret); it became what publishers today would hype as a 'number one best seller'. On this occasion it thoroughly deserved to be so regarded, for it is still in print in many languages throughout the world and almost every economics student hears of it (though few, too few, actually get round to reading it).

It is reported that when Mrs Thatcher became Prime Minister of Britain in 1979, her new Industry Minister, Sir Keith Joseph, sent copies of Adam Smith's classic book to his senior civil servants and suggested that they read it if they wanted to understand what the new Tory government's policies were to be about. It is not reported how many of them did so, though I suspect that there was a ready market for unofficial summaries along the lines of 'Bluff Your Way Through Adam Smith and Humour the Minister'.

The unique role of bargaining

Mrs Smith's son distinguished himself in his book by identifying a 'certain propensity' in human society to 'truck, barter, and exchange one thing for another'. His ideas on the significance of this propensity are worth considering.

First, he noted that the propensity to truck, barter and exchange was common to all people but was not to be found in any other species on the planet:

> 'Nobody', Smith wrote, 'ever saw a dog make a fair and deliberate exchange of one bone for another with another dog. Nobody ever saw one animal by its gestures and natural cries signify to another, this is mine, that yours: I am willing to give this for that.'

Bargaining is unique to the human species and it has a long pedigree back into the mists of time.

Second, he noted that people in any civilized society require the co-operation of others for their very survival and yet a person's 'whole life is scarce sufficient to gain the friendship of a few persons'. Think about that. How would you have fared if the services of the millions of people who have co-operated to produce just the goods and services that you have consumed this very day were withdrawn from your end of the market?

You would have had to feed yourself, provide for your own safety, perhaps cope with a medical problem, attend to your needs in every respect, and also think about what you have to do to ensure your survival tomorrow (and through tonight!). There is no doubt that, whatever else this would mean to you personally, it would certainly mean a drastic reduction in your standard of living, and, perhaps, a shortening of your life.

Friends always come in handy – a friend in need is a friend indeed – but the majority of people whom you depend upon for the many things you take for granted will never have time to get to know you, let alone get to know you in a way which makes them feel positive about helping you. Indeed, getting to know you might have the effect of encouraging entirely negative feelings towards you.

Third, Smith posed the question as to why people co-operate to produce things for people they will never meet, never know and probably would never like even if they knew them? Smith's answer was controversial. It still offends some people. He said that people co-operate not for love of their fellows, or indeed because of their humanity, but because it is in their *self-interest* to do so:

> 'It is not', he wrote in his famous assertion, 'from the benevolence of the butcher, the brewer, or the baker, that we expect our dinner, but from their regard to their self-interest.'

Self-interest
What is the nature of this self-interest? Quite simply it is people's desire for what you are going to give them in exchange for their meat, beer and bread. They certainly ain't going to give you their goods for nothing.

Relying on their benevolence will not loosen their hold on their meat, beer and bread sufficient to ensure you a long and contented life as much as will relying on offering them something in trade. In a contest between benevolence and trade as a motivator of human beings, it is more likely that trade will induce people voluntarily to part with what they have that you desire.

In effect, said Smith, you are showing them that parting with their wares in exchange for yours is to their own advantage – you are appealing, in other words to that most powerful of human motives: self-interest.

'Give me that which I want, and you shall have this which you want' is, for Smith and the majority of us, the one sure way to obtain the greater part of the things we are in most need of. This is the essential meaning of trading. And we trade by making offers and counter-offers, or bargaining.

All who produce anything that somebody else might want can participate in trade. Someone, somewhere, who wants what you have to trade can trade what they have for what they want, perhaps through long chains of intermediaries who know nothing about anybody one or two links along the chain in either direction, and thereby they can satisfy their desires without even knowing about you. It does not matter what kind of person you are, what race, nationality or religion you are blessed with, what your politics are, what your age, what your sex, or what your likes and dislikes.

If you engage in trade you become connected with those others who trade with you, and with the people who trade with them, in a world economic system that has raised living standards to levels undreamt of by Adam Smith and his contemporaries.

Smith's powerful insight into the propensity to truck, barter and exchange remains one of the most challenging concepts in business. Experience since 1776 suggests that those countries that live closer to the principles of free trade do better than those that have abandoned them.

Negotiating is the name of the game

If you want to trade you have to negotiate, or accept what the other guy offers. By negotiating you can improve on what you are first offered for what you have that the other guy wants. Smith certainly saw it that way: people truck, barter and exchange, they do not just accept what's on offer.

Negotiating is the name of the game. How to negotiate, how to get better deals, how to improve your share of the cake – how to get a bigger cake for both of you! – that's what this book is about. And more!

Trade is an international activity. Of the 160 countries in the world, all of them engage in trade, some more than others. This book is also about negotiating in some of the major trading countries of the world.

We look at what is appropriate in some trading regions of the world, what to do and what not to do: the you-better-believe-its and the no-nos.

Business methods and ethics can vary across the globe. If you want to do business in foreign lands and with foreign traders you must get acquainted with their differing styles and approaches. They are not going to change to suit you and your way of life: you must change or get out of the international trading business.

This book is about doing business *anywhere* and not just in your own backyard. If you feel safer by trading with Joe round the corner from your home, well and good. There is no compulsion on anybody to get into the international business scene: foreign trade is strictly for volunteers. But you owe it to yourself to look at the international scene before you dismiss it.

As with my other book, *Everything is Negotiable!*, this is a practical, not a theoretical, survey of the world of negotiating for business. I have packed in as much practical advice as the book can carry on the negotiating methods used by practical traders the world over. If the winners use these methods every day, you ought to learn about them now and use them immediately.

Negotiating has a basic structure the world over, but the practical principles – how and when the shots are played – varies from business culture to business culture. What might be regarded as a necessary display of aggressive pricing in the United States could be taken as the ultimate in bad manners in Saudi Arabia; the Japanese may react to your personal manner and its associated mannerisms in an entirely different way from the Soviet trade official; the 'leetle geeft for your wife' in the Philippines could get you hauled into a local court in France; and what is good for business and the country in Britain might be regarded as the height of inefficiency in Germany.

Hence, the text is littered with examples of the different, and sometimes subtle, ways in which the negotiating shots are played across the globe. It does not matter for what stakes you are negotiating, big or small, the examples cover the entire spectrum of deals from multi-million-dollar deals right down to the price of a taxi, or a drink or a copy of your favourite national newspaper at a news-stand in downtown Ogoland. Never neglect to look for lessons in every transaction you witness or participate in; they all have something to teach us about the business of trading.

Self-assessment tests
At the beginnings of Chapters 2 to 11 there is a short (and painless!) self-assessment test. Read the questions carefully and then mark

the answer that you consider to be most appropriate, given the information available.

As you read the chapter you will see how I have approached the negotiating issues raised in the questions. My opinions on the answers (with purely nominal scores) are set out at the end of each chapter. The opinions I express are, of course, entirely my own and you might feel that you have good cause to differ with them. You may question my opinions, and, indeed, anybody else's, on negotiating!

I believe that the views I have expressed on negotiating situations represent the 'best practice' for the majority of occasions I have chosen to illustrate in this way, but, as every negotiator knows, other people – sometimes the majority – see things differently from the way we do – that is why we need to negotiate! – so I am not going to be upset if you decide to differ.

At the Negotiating Clinics we have *lively* sessions when we discuss the answers that negotiators have chosen in contrast to mine. I am sometimes asked about the significance of the scores in the tests. Could I put it this way? The discussion of the answers is far more important than the size of your score, but if you get a high score in each test you can't be doing all that badly as a negotiator (though you might not realize that you can *always* do better), and if you get a low score, you know you have room for improvement, which may not be so obvious to the high scorer, and, in a way, this gives you an edge doesn't it?

Self-assessment test 1

1 You are negotiating with a team of engineers at a large turbine factory in Wusan, China. There are eight people on their side of the table and three on yours. Two of your colleagues are from corporate headquarters in Milwaukie. How many foreigners are at the meeting?
   - *(a)* 1?
   - *(b)* 3?
   - *(c)* 8?
   - *(d)* 10?

2 Just before you leave for a business trip to France, the British House of Commons passes (yet) another law with which you disagree completely. Over dinner in Paris you have an opportunity to make your views on this new law known to your hosts. Do you:
   - *(a)* Give them the benefit of your detailed opinions on why the law ought not to have been passed?
   - *(b)* Merely report the bare facts and give a single sentence argument for and then against the measure?
   - *(c)* Tell them that you know little more about the new law than you read in the French papers that morning?
   - *(d)* Tell them you have no views on the new law?
   - *(e)* Ask them how they see the new law?

3 You are waiting at Sharjah airport (United Arab Emirates) for a connection and an Arab passes in front of where you are sitting. A woman is following behind him and she has her face covered with a leather mask. Do you:
   - *(a)* Comment on this to the stranger sitting next to you?
   - *(b)* Say nothing about it, not even in response to the stranger's comments?

2 The worst thing you can do when abroad

or, foreigners, bloody foreigners

Bad manners

What is the worst thing that you can do when negotiating abroad? Quite simply it is to forget that it is you, not the other guy, who is the foreigner.

You are not in a foreign land – you are a foreigner in somebody else's homeland. The people there are not foreigners – they live there! You are the foreigner. You have the peculiar ways. You are the one out of step. You have the awkward mannerisms and you are the object of curiosity. If you start off thinking otherwise, you will probably take a lot longer than you needed, or expected, to get the business you feel you deserved.

To you, your country may be God's little Eden, the finest land in the world and worthy of the utmost respect from those not privileged to live in it. And your beliefs may be perfectly reasonable – to you. But, please, spare the people you travel the world to negotiate with your unsolicited and unrestrained eulogies about the land of your birth.

Not only is it bad manners to bore people with your fantasies, it can be downright insulting to be on the receiving end of someone's jingoistic ravings, and the implied manners (or lack of them) that are based on unblemished super-patriotism, especially when the other party might have similar deeply felt emotions about their own country.

Pride in one's country is one thing – and perfectly harmless if handled discreetly – but ramming your pride down the other guy's throat is altogether unacceptable, and, what is decisive, it is bad for business.

No matter where you come from on the planet, it is not the entire extent of the achievements of the human race. Other peoples, other places, other times, all make their contribution to human progress and civilization.

9

I knew a negotiator who, having had a rewarding and steady career as a buyer in Britain for a major international company, was sent to Italy to help integrate a newly acquired subsidiary into the European division. Although he had dealt with overseas agents for many years, his negotiating contacts with 'foreigners' had been largely conducted by telephone and telex.

Henry had not worked abroad before but head office had selected him for this temporary assignment because of his extensive experience as the company's buyer and also because he was near retirement and the posting would enable them to undertake some re-organization in the European division six months earlier than they had planned.

His successful completion of the assignment did not threaten anybody else's career progression (his absence, in fact, speeded up the promotion of several other executives), while failure was not expected, in view of his seniority and the relatively minor nature of the integration problems.

Within weeks, however, the spectre of a disaster materialized. That there was something going badly wrong with his assignment soon became apparent to London. They did not at first take the early reports too seriously, which was probably a mistake in retrospect, but eventually they decided that they had to act, though they were not keen to rush in and make changes without giving their much esteemed executive full benefit of their collective doubts.

They wanted an unbiased and independent report of what was going on, or, rather, not going on, and I was asked to take a look while I was passing through Italy on another assignment. On the basis of this report, if it was negative, they would recall their executive and replace him with somebody else.

The problem was essentially quite simple. Henry had got himself into a state by being extremely uptight about the Italian style of doing business – and style of doing anything else for that matter – which is, broadly speaking, one of emotional volatility and intense haggling. He regarded them as 'foreigners, bloody foreigners' and beyond redemption.

It started from the moment he picked me up at Galileo Galilei airport (Pisa) in his hired Mercedes. He moaned about right-side driving and Italian road manners all the way to Luca. In his office he went on and on about how long it took to get anything done. In his splendid villa, overlooking the Tuscany coast high in the mountains, he berated the work rate of the domestic staff employed to keep him comfortable during his stay.

It took considerable effort on my part to get him to talk about the operations of the new acquisition and what London wanted him to do that week, because he no sooner got going on any subject than he launched into another diatribe against the few real, but mainly imagined, faults of the Italians.

Over the days I was with Henry, he became speechless at the slightest slip in those around him; a delayed telephone connection, a misplaced memo or file, or the late arrival of a 'foreigner' to a meeting. I got the impression that he was obsessed with the trivial details of these events.

Faced with the usual harmless Italian chaos that passes for their sense of order, whether at a bank, government office, or agency, he would become almost apoplectic with rage. He did not confine himself to groaning to me privately about it. He entered the fray with a gusto, and could be seen gesticulating – in English! – just like an irate Italian at anybody he felt was guilty of being less than proper in their queue manners, or less than attentive to his needs.

I am sure he did not realize just how funny these scenes were and how ironic was his criticism of Italians when he acted like one!

His total lack of empathy with the 'foreigners' he was supposed to work with was dominating his entire life. He had forgotten what he was there for, which included getting on well with the local nationals who were to manage the subsidiary and integrate their operations into a European-wide business.

The amount of actual work he was required to do – including the review of previously negotiated finance and confirmation of partly concluded deals with suppliers in Turin and Milan – was a busy schedule for anybody giving it their best shot, but near impossible for somebody with neurotic attitudes to the Italian people, individually and collectively.

In fact, I was bound to tell London that his work rate was as bad as that of the Italians whom he criticized because he spent so much time criticizing them, and telling them how they did it much better in England, that neither he nor the people he was criticizing had much time left to do anything purposeful, except start over again where they last finished off with another bout of criticism.

A recall (with a generous early retirement) became inevitable. He did not fail because he was bad at his job as a manager of the

11

buying function. He failed because he was not very good at being a foreigner!

Now this does not mean that you should refrain from criticizing the country you are in and go to the other extreme of criticizing the country that you come from. Your negotiating partners are likely to consider you disloyal and insincere if you attack your own country in tones normally reserved for attacking somebody else's.

They will not regard you as other than fawning if you try to curry favour with them by behaving in such a way.

Franco wasn't funny

A colleague and I had occasion, not long after General Franco had died, to negotiate with a shipper in Barcelona, Spain, who wanted to import specialized steels from Britain. He thought that there was a market for such products and he believed (rightly) that Britain had a good reputation for technical excellence and sound quality in these particular steels.

Harry, my colleague, however, spent a lot of time at the evening meal late one night (and Spaniards, by the way, eat closer to midnight than to midday) knocking Britain for six.

It was not so much that Harry was knocking the country with which he expected the Catalunian importer to do business (itself remarkably inept as a negotiating behaviour), but that he was interspersing his derogatory remarks with fulsome, and extravagent, praise of Spain: 'How wonderful it must be to live in Spain, and how I wish I had been brought up here', he said repeatedly.

We almost lost the deal for this impertinence. The fact was that our Spanish host had suffered considerably for many years at the hands of Franco's corrupt and bullying local party bosses, and this alone indicated to him that my colleague did not know what he was talking about. If Harry had lived under a fascist dictatorship, instead of in a free country, he would have been more circumspect about criticizing Britain and praising Franco's Spain.

And on the aircraft home, Harry denounced the Spaniard for being ungrateful and giving us only a small first order. In the circumstances we were lucky to get even that.

Hence, be most careful how you behave as a foreigner. And get used to being one. In popular usage, a foreigner is somebody else; seldom do we see ourselves as foreigners, especially when we are abroad in another country.

Insensitivity

The apocryphal story of the Londoner stopped for speeding in Texas, deserves to be true. After a short conversation with the driver the Texan policeman asked him: 'Say, are you a foreigner?' To which the indignant Londoner replied: 'Certainly not! I'm British!'

Yet outside our own little backyards we are the foreigners. In fact we are foreigners to the vast bulk of the human race. We have the funny habits, the weird tastes and the strange mannerisms, which is why tourists come to gawp at us and to mimic our oddities.

When we leave our backyards and head for the rest of the world, we are the strangers in their land; it is not their land that is strange.

If you don't like foreigners, and cannot abide being one yourself, you are in the wrong business. In late-night wind-down sessions in bars and restaurants all over the world you will hear fellow negotiators from Britain, India, Pakistan, the USA and Australia, lay into the people they have been negotiating with that day, sometimes in the most patronizing, not to say racialist, of ways. (Interestingly, though my sample is small, I have never heard derogatory remarks of this nature from South Africans, though I have heard them complain bitterly about people who abuse them in public yet insist on negotiating with them for business in private.)

Having discussed the subject with many Third World negotiators, I can identify the national group who most wantonly display their assumed superiority (with an arrogance bordering on racism): they are in fact citizens of the Soviet Union and other East European communist states.

This behaviour does not endear them to the people they negotiate with in Third World countries, and it can bubble over into open friction. Even the 'fraternal' socialist regimes of Africa and Asia can become estranged from Great Russian nationalism posing as Soviet socialism. (I have no direct knowledge of how Cubans react to Soviet elitism, though I suppose it must irritate them too.)

Most negotiators, including the moaners mentioned above, manage to overtly control their feelings – most of the time! – during face-to-face sessions. Their inner feelings tend, however, to get an airing, often in loud emotional voices, when they join the company of other expatriates in their hotels.

Where their contempt for their opposite numbers is barely concealed, they are in great danger of not doing well in the negotiations. If offensive asides come across in contact with people

IVAN WAS NOT AMUSED

During a major negotiation with a Soviet trade delegation, the entire deal fell through due to the unfortunate remarks of one of the British members to the senior Soviet trade official over a glass or two of vodka in one of the informal sessions.

The British negotiator apparently had very strong personal views on the political (in)competence of Mrs Thatcher, and thought it appropriate to let his Soviet counterpart know how he felt about his country's Prime Minister (presumably on the grounds that because Mrs Thatcher has a reputation of being anti-communist he would be popular with the Soviet negotiators if he attacked her in public).

As it happens, nothing worries Soviet officials, at all levels of their country's bureaucracy, more than attacks on persons in authority. They get notoriously nervous about criticism of their leaders emanating from their own citizens (and punish it severely), and are both worried and embarrassed when they hear such criticism from foreigners.

'He called his own Prime Minister a poodle!', the Soviet negotiator told me privately. 'Who would want to do serious business with somebody who speaks of his country's leaders in that way?', he added. Hence, they didn't.

of the host nation, or their condescension secretes into their tones, they are bound to cause offence, and in doing so, jeopardize their business.

Today there is an extreme sensitivity across the globe to implicit, let alone explicit, affronts to national and personal pride. It may be that some of this sensitivity ought to be replaced with a sense of humour and a more sensible appreciation of the significance of those silly lapses in good manners (where they are lapses and not norms for behaviour).

Tired and emotional negotiators are boring wherever they come from, and so are their over-sensitive victims. But beware, what for you is passed off as a joke in bad taste might be enough in some parts of the world to get you jailed or deported (and perhaps worse).

We are the foreigners
For you, the need to appreciate your own foreignness is a

pre-condition for entering the world of international business negotiating.

Consider two linked questions: why do people live in different parts of the globe and not with you in your backyard?; why are they different from you?

The answers are not trite, for they draw out the essential truths that are no less important just because you take them for granted.

Different tribes of the human race live in different parts of the globe because their predecessors settled there and made a successful adaptation to local climatic and environmental circumstances.

They will pass on to their successors the most successful means for surviving in that part of the globe. In Greenland and northern Canada, Inuits (Eskimos) survive by adapting to the environment. In Indonesia, locals do likewise. The same is true across the entire spectrum of weathers, seasons, soils and sustenance.

Separating out that which is traditional and that which is modern (or international) in any society is a useful beginning for anybody contemplating a visit (especially one with commercial business in mind). For those who live in those parts, how they live and what adaptations they have made are perfectly natural and normal ways of behaving; so natural, in fact, that they regard your ignorance of them and their ways as a sign of *your* foreignness not theirs.

Hence, I can be specific: in a strange land it is not the land that is strange but you. You are the foreigner, not them. They live where they do because their predecessors discovered long ago how to live there successfully.

And in all cases it is not just a matter of climatic adaptation – the cultural, historical and political background has influenced the local approach to business.

The American who negotiates in Tokyo in much the same way as he does in Chicago will end up having to look for business elsewhere. The German who ships his goods to Egypt because his Arab counterpart said 'yes' to his proposition, might have to send them back again.

Pace the negotiations too fast in one culture and you'll get nothing for your pains, pace them too slow in another culture and you'll be pipped by the competition.

These kinds of negotiating errors are caused by forgetting your foreignness. You are on your own, perhaps thousands of miles from the part of the world that is most familiar to you, and you are bound to feel a trifle uneasy with your unfamiliar surroundings. You must realize, of course, that it is you that is unfamiliar, not the surroundings, for they have been there a long time.

So, if your foreignness leads you into error, you must invest some time and energy in compensating for it. You should make an effort to find out about the people with whom you want to do business.

You could do worse than start with learning a few of the polite greetings and salutations in the language of the country you intend to visit. If you are likely to spend any period of time in residence there you should be able to ally your stomach to the cause of learning and introduce yourself to at least restaurant level competence in the language.

Making an effort in this way will show your counterpart that you are less of a foreigner than someone who has not the slightest clue about the country's language. Becoming less of a foreigner is a small first step to showing respect for the people with whom you want to do business, and from mutual respect more than one good deal will follow.

If you are not yet convinced of this, you have already forgotten what Henry should have remembered: the worst thing you can do when negotiating abroad is forget that you are the foreigner.

Answers to self-assessment test 1

1   There are three foreigners at the meeting: yourself and your two colleagues from corporate headquarters. The eight Chinese citizens are local nationals and not foreigners. If you circled 3 take ten marks; for any other number deduct ten marks (and read Chapter 1!).

2   *(a)*   Not if you wish to develop a proper negotiating relationship with them. You have no idea of their views on the law (perhaps they support similar laws in France). It is best not to criticize your own country when abroad.   (-10)

     (b)   The very most you should ever do if you must comment at all, being particularly careful to inform them objectively rather than indicate your own views.   (3)

     (c)   Good avoidance move. Keeps you out of trouble and could be followed by *(e)* if you are pushed further.   (5)

(d) Safest move if you suspect the matter is controversial and are not sure of your host's views. (10)

(e) Good for stalling and gets them talking and you listening. (10)

3 (a) It is always pointless to criticize the customs of another country to a stranger. He could be a western-educated Arab who sounds like an expatriate and he might deeply resent what he regards as your ignorance or rudeness. How a country organizes its affairs is none of your business, if you really want to do any with them. (-10)

(b) Always the best policy. Airports and bars are full of wise guys who resent the countries they are in and people who live differently from themselves. They can get you into trouble and will bore you once they get your attention. Ignore them and their silly comments. (10)

Self-assessment test 2

1 You are about to leave home for a ten day selling trip to five major Canadian cities. Do you:
   - (a) Select enough clothes from your wardrobe to last the ten days, plus some extras in case you need them?
   - (b) Travel light, with what you stand up in, plus a single change of garments?
   - (c) Compromise between having every contingency covered and having no contingencies covered?

2 You run a consultancy in new technology and receive a telex inviting you to speak to a trade conference in Acapulco, Mexico. They ask for your fee and terms for participating. Do you:
   - (a) Go in at a nominal fee as you have not been to Mexico before and would like to visit Acapulco?
   - (b) Quote your standard fee and terms, and include first-class air travel?
   - (c) Ask them how many participants will be attending and what they are paying per head?

3 You are travelling to Sydney and get into conversation with a businessman in the next seat who is going as far as Bahrain. He asks where you are staying in Sydney and you reply 'the place I always stay, the Regent at Circular Key'. He advises you of a 'smashing hotel, the Corroberee'·he has discovered at the 'back of Kings Cross' and waxes on eloquently about it until the plane arrives at Bahrain. Before leaving he tells you to mention his name and introduce yourself to the hotel's owners 'Ben and Peggy', and assures you of an excellent place to stay. On arriving in Sydney do you:
   - (a) Take a look at the Corroberee?
   - (b) Take a taxi to the Regent?

3 The business of travel

or, if you enjoy it
you're obviously a tourist!

No romance here

Business travel is seldom romantic or exciting for those who often undertake it. Professional international negotiators regard travel as a chore that must be endured because it is a necessary part of the job. The suitcase life is by no means as glamorous as the stay-at-homes believe it to be. Those who suffer from crushed shirts or blouses, creased pants or skirts and stale socks or tights are unimpressed by the travel fantasies of those who do not.

Travelling occasionally as a tourist is all very well (and economical) if it is a prelude to spending a fortnight soaking up a lazy tan on a beach somewhere, but travelling regularly on business is an entirely different activity, especially when you have to perform brilliantly on arrival half-way round the world.

Travel is a chore whatever mode of transport you use. Travelling first or business class, instead of on a tourist cheapie, reduces the burden somewhat but does not eliminate it entirely. Jet lag does not defer to the class of travel that you use (quite the opposite if you over-indulge in the 'free' booze on offer in first and business class).

Overseas travel costs you more than the fare you pay: you suffer the inconvenience of the journey to and from the airports you fly from and to, the boredom of the flights in-between, and, perhaps, the follies of the hotels at which you stay.

Announcing your first visit to Hawaii to your friends may cause them to feel envious of your job, but if you arrive at Honolulu tired, dehydrated, and in a rain storm, collapse into a bedroom that is next to a noisy air-conditioning shaft, find that your luggage has been lost somewhere en route, and that your dearest wish is to sleep when you should be meeting the people you have come to see, you may decide that the experience is less than glamorous.

On your tenth visit to Hawaii (whatever you tell the guys in the office) you will view the long journey to get there with something less than enthusiasm, knowing that it will take just as long to get back. By your twentieth visit you will very likely feel it is time that somebody else undertook the chore.

Chore or not, there is no way that international business can be conducted without travel. The telephone is no substitute, nor is the telex, facsimile, video, or satellite hook-up. Sending a letter is not much better. You can effect an introduction by post, even make them an offer, but you cannot negotiate a complex deal, particularly if the option of getting off your perch and going out to see them is available. Bargaining without visual contact and close physical presence is a risky business when the stakes are high and the issues non-routine.

Long haul travel automatically involves air travel, and this means incarceration in a large cylinder that tunnels through the sky on eight- to ten-hour shifts (the airlines call them 'legs'). This need not induce serenity and peace. Apart from the squawking kids three rows along and the drunk next to you (or *vice versa*!), there is always the irritation of other people sitting between you and the cabin service.

On a long-haul flight (say, twenty-nine hours to Sydney) you know the difference between a jumbo with 315 people on board and one that is more than half empty. The service always grinds slowly towards you (or arrives just as you have got to sleep); it is a law of travel that no matter where you sit, the cabin service always starts somewhere else!

The best you can do is to make your entire journey as comfortable as possible. This means going first or business class. Money is never 'saved' by going economy or tourist class. If you are more tired than you need to be because you tried to skimp on the air fare, it could cost your company more than the money they 'save' sending you economy.

On lugging your luggage

The next target for your attention ought to be your luggage. Most people take far too much with them and the more they take the more they have to carry and be responsible for.

Why business negotiators travelling, not to the outposts of Ogoland, where little of what they might need is available to them, but to the richer parts of the globe, pack enough shirts to change more than once a day and enough suits and accessories to last an

A TICKET IS NOT A SEAT

Ticketing is an art form. Ordering an air ticket is only the first step towards getting on to the aircraft. They still have to get the tickets into your hands which can be easier said than done.

I once ordered a ticket from Edinburgh to Nairobi which had not arrived the day before my journey. The agency assured me that they had sent it to me the same day I ordered it. Despite several phone calls about the missing ticket they did not mention by which means they had sent it and I assumed it was via the GPO. In the end I faced having to purchase another ticket from a local agent at full fare and, in desperation, rang the local rail station in case it had been sent by 'Red Star'. Sure enough, my ticket was at the station and had been there for a week!

Getting your ticket and yourself to the airport does not necessarily get you on to an aircraft. The airlines reserve the 'right' (it's outright impudence in fact!) to 'over-book' each flight. This could leave you standing at the check-in with your travel plans in ruins.

I was denied boarding at Amman (Jordan) because the check-in computer said the plane was full, even though I patently was the first passenger in the line. After vigorous protests and much confusion, they discovered a computer malfunction: it had listed every seat as being occupied by the same passenger, a Mr O'Shaunnesy – a cousin of the famous Mr Murphy? – who in the event didn't even turn up!

You could even get on the aircraft and still get chucked off.

I witnessed a woman being put off an aircraft about to depart for New Zealand, having been issued with a boarding pass and allowed on with the rest of the passengers, because the airline did not discover it was over-booked until there was one passenger left standing after everybody else had sat down. Thank goodness she was not Miss World or royalty, as they might have chucked me off instead! *(Moral: if you get on board, get seated, strapped-in, stuck into your newspaper, and don't look up until take off.)*

entire season baffles me, though it was an apparent stroke of ill-luck that wakened me up to the idiocy of these ways.

On a flight to London from Sydney my luggage was lost. Naturally, I was not very pleased with this occurrence and waxed long and loudly on the theme of changing the airport's name from Heathrow to Thiefrow, which could have offended the good men and women of London's busiest airport, but I hope that they put my wild allegations down to jet lag and the time in the morning. (I did not dare make any reference to the possibility that the luggage was 'lost' at Sydney – they have grounded the likes of Frank Sinatra there for 'insulting' remarks he is alleged to have made and I can't even sing!)

I only had the fairly crumpled suit and shirt I was wearing and my first appointment was in two hours. What to do? Obviously I had to acquire some replacement clothes. And this opened my eyes. There are hundreds of places to buy inexpensive clothes in cities like London. A quick visit to Marks and Spencers (or the overseas equivalent) will soon produce a most presentable outfit.

It occurred to me: why do I insist on carrying all this luggage about at risk to my health and temperament when I can purchase what I need on arrival?

The answer eventually became a way of life for me when I travel. I decided there and then to travel light, supplementing anything I have not brought with a quick purchase locally.

For a two week trip you are unlikely to need anything more than you can get into a regulation size cabin bag (450 × 350 × 150mm or 18 × 14 × 6 ins). Women should note that they have the privilege of being able to add their handbags to the cabin bag allowance. This suggests that they should take a large handbag – and that men should stuff their pockets with odds and ends!

If when you pack your cabin bag you find that you still want to take more possessions, I suggest that you are taking too much. Empty it out and be more ruthless.

I have found it useful to wear my business suit jacket on to the plane with a pair of lightweight casual trousers. My suit trousers are neatly folded in the bag and, once on the plane, I neatly fold my suit jacket into the overhead locker. On a business trip round Europe I appeared neatly turned out at all times using combinations of three pairs of lightweight trousers and a single blazer – dark trousers for more formal sessions and light trousers for relaxation.

The rest of the bag is for accessories. What I take I wash and iron at the hotel (of which more in a moment) and if I need something else I simply buy it locally.

If you are unconvinced of the virtues of this policy, ask yourself what you intend to do with all the shirts and underwear you insist on carrying: are you intending to spend your trip lugging round a pile of dirty washing?

If you balk at carrying dirty washing, you must intend to get them cleaned as you go, and, if this is the case, you can cut down on the number of shirts (blouses) by using the same-day service at your hotels. Clothes sent for cleaning in the morning are ready for you by 6 p.m. (or you are in the wrong hotel!).

Its also better to send a steady stream of single items to the cleaners rather than pile it together to make a load – you never know when an emergency might strike and you need a quick change. Accidentally spilt soup or booze, a sudden tear or an unexpected invitation to dinner or an appointment can catch you out if your only other clothes are waiting to go to the laundry.

You can buy low-priced shirts and such-like almost anywhere, to supplement what you have brought. I am sometimes asked what happens if you buy locally and then have to carry it all home? That depends on whether you want to take it home. You can throw items away!

Why balk at throwing away a cheap shirt you wore only once for a specific purpose connected with your business when you think nothing of spending five or more times what the shirt cost on a meal or entertainment? Both activities are related to your business and you should be philosophical rather than neurotic about their worth.

On the toiletries front the same rules apply. True you can get an ingenious adapter that enables you take electrical appliances with you and use them almost anywhere in the world. You can also get battery versions of shavers, curlers, hairdryers and toothbrushes too. But why carry them with you when you risk losing them en route, or having them fail for some reason?

Everything you need (including simple throwaway wet shavers and toothbrushes) in the way of soaps, shampoos, perfumes, after-shaves, talcs, hairsprays and toothpaste is always available at hotel shops, so why carry them? You can carry an emergency supply if your security level bothers you, but make sure it is a miniature supply and not enough to see you through a long prison sentence.

As for towels and facecloths, you have no reason to assume that your hotel does not have them freely available (unless these are for you what child psychologists call 'security blankets'). Of course, in some parts of the world it would be an unsafe assumption to expect to find accessories freely available, but in North America, Europe, Australia, Japan, Latin America and South Africa, it is silly to pay for hotel services that include towels etc. and still insist that you lug your own about as well.

Naturally, your bag will contain your business papers, and these should also be kept to a minimum. Whatever your intentions, it is unlikely that you will work through as much of your office papers as you think on your journey. I am not at all convinced that you should take your office work with you anyway. It is a myth of the busy (read disorganized) executive to believe that he or she will use the flight time and the evenings in the hotel to sort through company budget accounts, reports from other sections, quotations for other contracts, and overdue reports for the boss.

The truth is (and I have checked this by asking executives to be candid about their use of time on overseas trips) that you will only half-heartedly look at those office papers during the flight and you will probably be too tired to look at them in the evenings. And if you do look at them you will only worry about the obvious things that should be done and waste a lot of time thinking about not being able to do them. Mostly, they will only add weight to your luggage.

A major advantage of the single regulation-size cabin bag on an international trip is that you eliminate at a stroke the anxiety of searching the baggage reclaim area for your other cases (another law of business travel says that your luggage is never first off the reclaim track). Waiting for your luggage can add an hour to your journey time at most airports, especially when two or three jumbos are decanting their luggage into the same space.

Apart from the risk of your luggage being mislaid, it can be stolen. Some victims of theft ask for it. If you display your affluence by using well-known credit card luggage labels you ought not to complain if thieves make a beeline for the obvious honey pot.

With hand baggage only, you are bound to be among the first through customs and immigration and first to the taxis. You should be booking into your hotel while the rest of them are lugging their cases up the ramps to the customs hall. You could be showering, or sampling a Martini by the pool side, while they are fighting for a taxi and joining the mass scrum at reception.

Hotels

Hotels are another fact of business life for the international negotiator. They can either help or hinder your trip. So the best advice is not to skimp on them in a futile search for economies. Where you can you should stay in the four- or five-star type, preferably one that is part of an international hotel chain (Hyatt, Hilton, Intercontinental, Holiday Inn, Sheraton, Forte, Westin, and so on).

My reason for advising thus is quite simple: you know what you are getting for what you pay in the chain hotel. A negotiator does not have time for cultural immersion on a business trip. He or she does not have time to seek out the 'quaint' and the 'ethnic' during the few hours available for bed and relaxation. It is best to trust to the familiar rather than risk the unfamiliar (and 'tips' from people who stayed at this or that unusual hostelry off the beaten track should seldom be trusted and even less often acted upon – if it is that good they should keep it to themselves!).

The advice of old hands can often be useful, but be warned that the world's aircraft are full of people who like to give the impression that they are old hands in this or that place. Their ideas on what constitutes good service or adequate plumbing will more than likely qualify them for a PhD in eccentricity. They may not require first-class telephone links and top-rate reception services.

A chain hotel generally has the capacity to put things right if something is wrong. A Sheraton in Connecticut once changed my room merely because I mentioned to reception that the television was not working properly, while Hyatt, in San Francisco, gave me a suite instead of a room because they took so long to pick me up at the airport.

Negotiators working away from their home base need good communications and this means plenty of phone or telex lines (preferably with direct dialling facilities) at your disposal. Though watch those hotel charges for calls – they are positively lethal unless you negotiate a standard telephone company rate for all your calls, which you can do if you regularly use an international chain for your hotel requirements.

Never underestimate the value of a decent phone service. It used to be near impossible to do business in France because of its phone system. Instant access to your office (or your home) can be a soothing balm when you are under pressure. Small hotels have

TAXI!

A word, by way of a warning, about airport taxi touts. They must be avoided at all costs. Most airports have prominently displayed notices warning visitors not to get into anything other than an official taxi, and the local police often take the view that if you ignore specific warnings the consequences are none of their business.

At some airports they even hand out printed warnings about taxi touts to visitors as they move through immigration.

Many years ago, as a teenager passing through Colombo, in what has since been re-named Sri Lanka, I was ripped-off by a taxi tout who pretended to know the person I was supposed to be meeting; he told me, would you believe, that he had been sent to pick me up by this person! It cost me the equivalent of a month's wages for a Sri Lankian labourer for the ride but it taught me to avoid the touts who plague every airport.

People who ignore the warnings are damn fools. Only my policy of absolute non-interference in the education of those who need experience has prevented me from reminding those about to be led off by what is patently a taxi tout. They will find that the run from Leonardo da Vinci airport (Rome) will cost them the price of a week's stay at a city hotel – the experience will be salutary.

The police will not come to your rescue (except if physical violence is involved) when it comes to paying the tout's charge. At most you might haggle the price downwards a little – but if you haggle with taxi touts why did you get into the mess in the first place?

In some cities you can do a deal with a licensed taxi driver. You will be offered a half or quarter price run to the airport provided you let them take more than one fare (in Greece, taxis automatically seek more than one fare, often without asking you!). I agreed to this on one occasion in New York and the driver went off to look for another customer at the air terminal. Unfortunately he was unable to find anybody wanting to go out to Kennedy at that time. But a deal being a deal (after all he was a New York cabbie) he took me to Kennedy off the meter for a flat fare of $6.

inadequate phone facilities – some in the hall not in the room, which can be off-putting when you have confidential business to discuss.

Recently, I was stymied from getting my office to do a credit check on a client in up-country Australia because the phone was not just in the hall, it was within earshot of the bar where my client was sitting sipping his beer!

Large hotels note the numbers that you ring, in case of dispute. If this could embarrass you, use the call box instead.

Hotel chains tend to be more secure from the attention of thieves. How much you worry about theft depends on what you are carrying and when you were last a victim of crime. If you have never experienced theft of your possessions you will probably not take precautions, until some unknown thief educates you. Remember, there is nothing sacred about your wallet or passport or handbag.

In a different environment you may relax about things because you never worry about them at home. I know a copper buyer who had his trousers stolen on his first night in Zambia – they left behind his wallet which was on the dressing table. In Britain, Sir Geoffrey Howe, the then Chancellor, had his trousers and their contents (£50) stolen from his locked sleeping compartment on a train travelling at 100 miles an hour across normally law abiding Britain!

Thieves steal things in order to sell them. Your business papers will probably be dumped as worthless (unless the theft is aimed at industrial espionage or the nature of your papers leads to an opportunistic bit of the same). Hence, separate your papers from your case, though beware of the risks in doing so.

I stayed at the Post House, Heathrow, the week that it opened and placed my papers by the bed. When I returned at midnight I found that my possessions, such as they were, had been removed and incinerated by the maid who thought that I had checked out as she could see no case in the room. The management grovelled, profusely, of course, and I (or rather they) had to replace my shirt, socks and pants before breakfast, but I had to work without my papers and notes for the rest of the week.

In sum, be security conscious. Lock your door. Use the spy-glass in the door to check who is knocking. Place valuables in the hotel safe and generally make it difficult for thieves to get at your possessions – they will prefer to spend their time liberating the possessions of those who are careless with them.

Twenty cents is no rip-off

Another advantage of a chain hotel is that they generally provide, at a price, of course, banking services. I know that they charge for this service, especially when changing currency, but I doubt whether the percentage differences in currency charges are really worth the fuss that some people make about them. A couple of cents per pound sterling might matter if you are changing several thousand dollars, but hardly matter when it's a twenty dollar bill.

For some people, getting two cents to the pound less from the hotel bank than you can get downtown appears to cause more heartache (and longer boring speeches at the bar) than the fifty per cent mark up on the bar bill. I've seen supposedly serious negotiators reduced to grievous apoplexy over an alleged currency rip-off at reception, involving perhaps the 'loss' of fifty cents in total across the entire transaction. Yet these same 'business' professionals will willingly pay the same hotel ten pounds for a bottle of wine that costs two pounds in the local supermarket.

If they ever thought about the mark-up they pay on hotel food (I've heard it can be over 4000 per cent in some places) they might take a more relaxed view of the 'rip-offs' in the Bureau de Change, and, more important, they might spare us all the dubious pleasures of listening to their outrage.

In summary then, this is my advice to the business traveller about to embark on his or her first 100,000 miles:

- Fly first- or business class on all trips – if your company argues, you are working for the wrong company.
- Restrict your luggage to a single carry-on cabin bag (plus a handbag if you are a woman, and full pockets if you are a man).
- Stay only at top-class or international chain hotels.
- Praise every display of good service and suggest a remedy for any let-down you experience.
- Reduce jet lag by adjusting your watch to the local time of the country you are visiting, avoid alcoholic drink on the flight but take plenty of other liquids, and go to bed only when the locals do.
- Only use official taxis, keep your valuables in a safe place, and if held up by a mugger give over what he wants without arguing – your life is worth more than whatever possessions you are carrying.

Answers to self-assessment test 2

1 *(a)* This must be your first trip otherwise you would have more sense. (-10)

   (b) By far the most sensible choice. Light travellers have less to worry about, get off the plane and through customs quicker, find it easier to make their way from hotels to airports and can get around the airport so much easier. (10)

   (c) Better perhaps than *(a)* but it depends towards which end of the spectrum you compromise. (5)

2 *(a)* You are not a serious business negotiator if you allow your personal desires to interfere with your commercial judgement. If you rationalize this answer right through you will probably do the trip for nothing, or, worse, offer to pay half of your costs just to get to Mexico! (-20)

   (b) Clearly you are not intimidated by the alleged romance of far away places, though you ought to ask for details as in *(c)* first. (5)

   (c) Much better. The more information you acquire the better. They may fill a stadium full of people wanting to know about new technology and your rate could work out at two cents per head, making your fee look ridiculous. (10)

3 *(a)* Advice about local hotels is almost always not worth acting upon. If the Corroberee is not to your taste you have the hassle of moving out. Ben and Peggy may have suited your companion but may be a pain in the neck to you. (-10)

   (b) Always your best bet if you are satisfied with the hotel you normally use (and you should be happy at the Sydney Regent, but don't take my word for it!). (10)

Self-assessment test 3

1 Your company is anxious to develop overseas markets for its high technology products. A Soviet representative invites you to Moscow to discuss a possible contract to supply a complete production system. Which of the following is likely to be the most difficult point to negotiate in the opening sessions:

    (a) Price?
    (b) Technical specifications?
    (c) Delivery?
    (d) Performance standards?
    (e) Export licences?
    (f) Methods of payment?

2 Your opposite number from the Soviet negotiating team is polite but otherwise cool. Do you:

    (a) Try to develop a personal relationship?
    (b) Treat with respect but keep your distance?

3 The Soviet negotiator tells you that they are having parallel negotiations with your major competitors, and you know this to be true because your rivals are sharing the same hotel and restaurants. He insists on price concessions from you to match those offered by the competition. Do you:

    (a) Agree if it still leaves the deal in profit?
    (b) Decline unless your prices can take a cut?
    (c) Offer some other concession instead?
    (d) Refuse to budge on price?

4 Negotiating with the (Russian) comrades
or, safety in buck passing

The monopoly of foreign trade

Trading with communist countries is as different as a hammer is from a sickle, and there is no way you can get into this relatively lucrative activity in the same way that you would bust into the US market. It is therefore a useful place to begin the main theme of this book.

For a start, the Soviets do not believe (officially at least) in the free market (or free much else) and they will certainly cast a jaundiced eye over you at Sheremetyevo airport, Moscow, if you turn up on a speculative visit hoping to sell a million gross of tapped holes to the manager of the local dynamo factory.

The Soviet market is not like any you have dealt with in the West and you could save yourself a lot of bother by finding out just how different it is before you get your visa from Ivan, your local Soviet consul; don't wait until you are slurping your borsch in Leningrad.

Put simply, the Soviet state jealously guards its monopoly of foreign trade, and everything, but everything, must go through official, and bureaucratic, channels; nothing is imported, or exported, at the whims of individuals, be they ever so powerful.

The system of control is all pervasive and there is precious little hope of getting round it with the usual dodges used by those in a hurry to enrich themselves. You will bend to the Soviet system of the state monopoly of foreign trade or you will not trade with them at all. It's as simple and as brutal as that.

If a manager in the Soviet or East European socialist system wants to acquire machinery for some purpose connected with the planned output targets assigned to his plant, he doesn't simply check the catalogues of suppliers of such machinery, invite them to send proposals, and then meet with their sales personnel for preliminary discussions. And even if, for some reason, he did do it this way, he cannot initiate a purchase by opening negotiations with the supplier while clearing the finance with his board of directors. He has to go through channels.

All industrial and commercial decisions are subject to planning from the top and, in the absence of a market, all decisions are made by bureaucratic means in the numerous administrative levels that plan, manage and review all economic activity in the Soviet Union.

Industrial Ministries supervise the work of product groups and their associated research and development projects, and State Committees co-ordinate overlapping interests and developments. To acquire imports of machinery and such-like, these organizations must work through the Ministry of Foreign Trade, which operates Foreign Trade Organizations (FTOs) in parallel with the Industrial Ministries and, in some cases, major industrial plants.

The negotiating process between the Western supplier and the actual end-user of its products has to work through these numerous levels of decision-making and the various strands of the bureaucratic system of Ministries, State Committees, and Foreign Trade Organizations. You cannot short-circuit the system and go straight to the end-user for a decision to buy. Indeed, it is unusual for a supplier ever to meet with the end user (which creates its own complications as we shall see).

Have you got the picture? Well, just to confuse matters, the system changes regularly, the extent to which its strictures and procedures are applied vary, and experience shows that on occasion the system will leap over normal sequences and produce a 'quick' decision. As you will never know when this is likely to happen, or why (perhaps somebody is covering for somebody else who, back along the line, has made a cock-up of some kind), you ought not to rely on it happening to you.

Getting business from the Soviets
There are various ways in which you might get into trading with communist states. You could be a sub-contractor to a Western supplier who holds a contract with the relevant Soviet department. If you are, your negotiating will be confined to the deal you make with the major contractor; but some aspects of their requirements will reflect the nature of their deal with the Soviets. You might find that they require considerable technical detail from you; this is a feature of Soviet type contracts.

You might be approached by a representative of a Soviet Trade

Mission (STM). The UK STM is a very large operation indeed and scans British industry from an impressive modern office block in Highgate in London. From there, Soviet specialists constantly sift through the technical press, attend exhibitions, launches, presentations and such-like. They look for products that might match Soviet needs. They act as the official link between you and the end-user, and they might supervise the entire negotiation or merely introduce you to the next layer of principals in the bureaucracy they represent.

Another way into the Soviet market is via the services of an agent specializing in communist markets. He finds a Soviet, or an East European, manufacturer who is looking for a machine to do a particular job and matches it with your company's products. He may initiate the enquiry with you on speculation or act as a searcher of business for you on regular tours of potential customers.

For this service, and for carrying you through the process of negotiation, which could last anything up to two years, he would get a percentage of the gross value of the order (say, 4.5 per cent).

You could also send a representative as part of a delegation touring the Soviet Union and Eastern Europe, perhaps organized by the local Chamber of Commerce, or by a government department, or your trade association, or you could exhibit at a trade fair.

The one thing you are most unlikely to do is to wander round the Soviet Union at will, looking for business, as you might wander round Germany or France.

Technical obsessions
Soviet trade negotiators are professionals, not enthusiastic amateurs. They prepare thoroughly and are well briefed and their internal systems compel them to act in ways that force you to disclose a great deal more than is normal in Western negotiations, especially in the technical aspects of the products involved.

The obsession with technical data of Soviet negotiators is not surprising if the industrial and political structure of their society is taken into account.

In the absence of price and competition as an indicator and regulator of quality, it is necessary for something to replace these roles, otherwise resources would be mismatched and inputs chosen arbitrarily. Communist societies replace the market as the arbitrator of demand and supply with committees of bureaucrats using various output indicators (tonnes, metres, cubic volumes etc.) in place of monetary values (though they do not always by any means totally avoid the mismatch of resources to needs and their economies can be very inefficient as a result).

Soviet officials are charged with checking the suitability, reliability and quality of purchases, and they take full responsibility for their decisions. Hence, they are careful; they work not to hunches and entrepreneurial initiatives but are risk-averse and routine-minded.

In other words, they check everything and require evidence for their records that they have checked everything, and these can be used to check on them by other committees whose sole job is to see that everything has been checked by those reporting to them.

Your negotiations are likely to be divided into two main stages: first, the assessment of technical competence of the product you are selling and what commitments they can extract from you in these qualifying negotiations, and secondly, the negotiations on the terms under which you will trade.

Great care is needed by negotiators in both phases because while the Soviet state is a 'good payer', as bankers put it, there is a *caveat* to their soundness as debtors: they pay promptly only if the terms of the contract are strictly met by the supplier.

If you accept loose undertakings in the performance negotiations you may live to regret their literal interpretation by faceless bureaucrats or end-users at a later stage. The Soviet official regards the contract as a sacred document and will operate it to the letter if it suits his interests.

If you say your machine can work under any temperature because you have never heard of a problem arising from the temperature range common to your own country, remember, some bureaucrat in an office in Omsk, on the basis of what he considers is a contractual obligation, may send your machines to a factory in Yakutsk, in deep Siberia. If your product freezes at twenty below zero and stops a production line, which prevents that plant meeting its quotas (or plausibly can be blamed for doing so), he will demand recompense; and nobody claiming compensation ever asks for small amounts! So if your payments are held up while you explain what you meant by 'any temperature', don't forget to kick yourself for being careless.

Get the contract right

The worst thing you can do is oversell your product to a communist

34

bureaucrat. They are held mercilessly liable for their own contractual agreements as state suppliers to end users. You can get an idea of the standard Soviet attitude to performance contracts from a statement by one of them in the aircraft industry in respect of his customers:

> 'After considerable negotiations with the customer as to what will be produced, the designer signs the contract and symbolically hands over his testicles with the contract. When the aircraft is delivered as specified, he gets his testicles back.'

All their negotiators are committee men and women brought up in a world where everything they do is covered by paperwork and they won't do much for you unless they get it written down. If you are careless with your commitments you might as well hand over whatever is for you the biological equivalent of your testicles.

Failure to deliver as promised (whether in time, quality or quantity) is endemic in the Soviet bureaucratic economy and much time is spent by managers (and their 'fixers') tirading against each other's failures and attempting to shift the blame elsewhere – this is where paperwork is worth its weight in buck-passing.

If there was a free legal system in the USSR, lawyers would be making small, and not so small, fortunes suing for alleged breaches of contract all over Soviet industry, and, whereas there are other than monetary sanctions on Comrade Ivan, against you they have a financial one, and if they don't have that for some reason, under their state monopoly of all trade they have the final one of total exclusion from their markets, for ever.

So get your performance contract precisely right. Specify exactly what your product can do and make no commitments that you cannot be absolutely sure your product can deliver. Under no circumstances slip in 'extras' that Western well-stocked engineering departments could cope with but which might be beyond actual Soviet practice to handle in less well-stocked or outrightly primitive plants run by crews who are less than enthusiastic about standards, particularly if they are not well motivated under their payments systems.

On their side of the table they will bring in high quality engineers to go over your product's specifications, most with names as confusing to remember as those in Tolstoy's novels (each representing some bureaucratic interest in their confusing management structures).

ON-SITE INSPECTION? NOT IN THIS COUNTRY, COMRADE!

A British manufacturer of welding equipment was surprised to receive a large bill from a Soviet customer for the repair of some of its machines. Not only was the charge excessive – you could almost buy the equipment new at that price – but the alleged fault had been identified by their own engineers many years previously as one caused by operator misuse.

In subsequent discussions with the Soviet Foreign Trade Organization responsible for the end-user's product group, the British negotiators insisted on the source of the problem and drew their counterparts' attention to the extremely detailed operating manual that warned specifically against certain operator practices and explained what would happen unless they followed precise instructions when switching off the equipment.

This was to no avail. The Soviet officials pressed for penalty payments under the terms of the orginal contract and insisted that the repair costs were not excessive.

In response to this deadlock, the British team insisted on inspecting the equipment. This was immediately rejected by the Soviet negotiators, on the grounds that there was nothing in the contract about on-site inspection.

The British refused to pay for repairs that they disputed, especially when they were denied access for inspection by their own engineers.

The problem lay in the contract terms. Unless it specifies for on-site inspection in cases of dispute it is unlikely that the Soviet officials will vary its terms retrospectively. Their total sensitivity about on-site inspection in the arms negotiations is replicated in commercial dealings unless you insist on it from the start.

Remember: what you sign you live with – or without, as the case may be.

It is no good saying that you have explained it all before and they can refer to the previous committee for details; your listeners will have come from a different interest group and will not be impressed or influenced by the statements of administrative units several layers, or several structures, away from their own (think of it from their point of view: the other lot may drop them in the proverbial fertilizer, so they must check for themselves before they sign anything at their level).

You must, therefore, be prepared for repetitive and intensive bouts of explanation, promotion and negotiation on technical aspects of your products, perhaps over several months, and you must not get wearied by this exhausting procedure (or if it does weary you, try another market!).

If you are not technically qualified to answer searching interrogations of your product's performance – and sometimes your questioners will seem like off-duty staff from the KGB's Lubyanka prison – you must get a technical specialist from your company sent along with you.

Penalty clauses

This is especially important when negotiating penalty clauses, which can be seen as the individual Soviet bureaucrat's insurance policy against being held responsible for failures; with a battery of penalty clauses general enough to cover almost everything that can go wrong, he can cover himself against criticism and protect his job (which at his level will accord him and his family important privileges).

The Soviet negotiator will try to get a penalty clause agreed that protects him against you not delivering on time – you should hold back any startling concessions on this point and certainly avoid a commitment to deliver to the site in the Soviet Union on time, as you are in the hands of British dockers, foreign seamen, foreign dockers and foreign railways (and all of them influenced by communists!).

Delivery should either be ex works (yours not theirs), to the gates of a UK port, or, *in extremis*, alongside the Soviet ship.

If you recklessly show signs of weakness here (i.e. concede too much too fast) they might try for a penalty clause for failing to send the associated documentation to them! And why not? The bureaucrat is concerned more with paperwork than the actual goods which are a problem for some other bureaucrat.

But the penalties will not stop there, if they can force you to concede more. The engineers who are concerned with the goods will require their negotiators to enforce a penalty for any delays in commissioning the plant.

Beware: you may not be solely responsible for when these plants are commissioned, though your contract might imply this. The Soviet system uses ranks of inspectors who specialize in checking on everything, including on each other – and sometimes, including the parts that are pre-assembled inside the machine (they might insist that you strip it down, even when the parts are sealed in!) – and you can rapidly commit your company to all kinds of penalties (or other pressures) by ill-considered concessions on commissioning dates.

The problem of inspection can be partly obviated by having their inspectors visit your plant to do some of their work while the machinery is under assembly. In this case you must make them responsible for the travel and subsistence costs of their inspectors!

Soviet inspectors require an excessive quantity of documentation related to imports – so much is required that it creates a suspicion that it is used for other purposes, such as an unauthorized (that is, unpaid for) transfer of Western technology.

They will want detailed workshop drawings (including part-assembly and mountings), lists of parts (down to washers and bolts), the test procedures and how they are to be conducted, certificates of the materials used (even chemical and other analyses), photographs of the plant (from all angles and not just those supplied in your brochures), full technical specifications of everything (and they mean *everything*!), full maintenance manuals (in Russian if they can get it), detailed information – including drawings – of parts that are expected to wear out, and certificates for welding and other work not open to test once delivered.

In return for this plethora of detail, you will find them less than efficient in getting information to you from their side, particularly the end-user's requirements or operating conditions. There is not a lot you can do about this other than wait, having made certain that your contractual obligations on delivery dates are not triggered until you receive essential details from them, and are time-suspended if there are delays emanating from their side. Do not underestimate the problems of delays caused by the Soviets themselves. These are legendary, such as when technical specifications arrive later than promised, their inspectors turn up a fortnight after they are supposed to have left their own country, and when they leave a week before they should have, with parts coming off the line which they were meant to inspect, and so on.

You are bound to be fairly confident in making a penalty commitment in the area of reaching promised quality and quantity targets – after all, you are in the business of supplying high quality products.

You should, however, be able to anticipate the negotiating line that is often taken by the buyer (and not just Soviet ones): 'If the quality and quantity claims you make for your machines are true, you will have no reason to fear agreeing to a penalty clause if these promises are not met?'

This could be game, set and match, if you fall for this without being very sure to have precise responsibilities demarcated – you guarantee the quality and quantity levels of output (and things like energy consumption, waste levels, noise or emission levels etc.) from your machines, if, and only if, the inputs are of a very closely specified quality (which they must guarantee to you) and the operators are fully competent and properly trained (which they must also guarantee to you) and the general working environment is suitable (which they must agree to provide).

At the very least, you will require site inspection rights by your engineers, not theirs, of your machines and how they are used in normal working sessions. And you had better get it agreed what they mean by a 'normal working session' if you are required to guarantee performance for a time period.

You might assume single-shift five-day working and give a two-year guarantee only to discover later, when parts are worn out, that they are working three shifts over six days (fairly standard practice) and thereby decreasing the duration of any performance guarantee you should give.

If you don't ask questions, even obvious ones, don't take umbrage when you realize later that you should have.

Take care to get included in the contract the right to revise all penalty dates once any one of them slips, otherwise they will not agree to do so later, and you are liable to be clobbered right through the life of the deal. Soviet officials seldom entertain variations in the terms of a contract once it has been agreed, so either get it right from the start, or don't sign it.

Performance negotiations with the Soviets can be harrowing,

WHO'S SORRY NOW?

The Soviet fad for penalty clauses is unbounded by any consideration for who might be to blame for the failure to reach promised (and perhaps, normal) performance standards. Unless, that is, you specifically insist on qualifying your promises with a clause in the contract to exclude your liability if the failing is in any way connected with the user's practices.

Legal experts on Soviet contracting practice suggest that something like the following is included in the contract that you sign (if it isn't, you ought not to sign – but, if you do, you should file your contract in the 'I'm-going-to-be-sorry' drawer!):

'(We) warrant that the technical documentation to be supplied will permit the licensee to manufacture, to the extent and under the conditions herein stated, products having the characteristics specified in the Schedule (attached) provided that (a) licensee complies with all technical standards, instructions and recommendations from licensor; (b) the machinery, tools and equipment used by the licensee are in conformity with the technical documentation furnished; (c) the parts and materials used by licensee in the manufacture of products meet the requirements specified in the technical documentation furnished; (d) the resources and skills applied by licensee to the manufacture of the product are those of a manufacturer experienced in the manufacture of a product of similar complexity and manufacture; and (e) the design of the product conforms exactly to the design furnished by the licensor (T. W. Hoya and D. D. Stein, 'Drafting Contracts in US–Soviet Trade', *Law and Policy in International Business*, vol. 7, p. 1087 (1975).

unless you regard these sessions as opportunities to concentrate entirely on your product's technical soundness and not as impertinent challenges to your company's reputation.

This is a dangerous time for you, and, under pressure, perhaps to impress your opposite number with the high quality of your company's products, you may be trapped into claiming it can do more than you should.

Aggressive sales patter sounds great at gung-ho presentations when an exaggerated claim ('this machine is so good it can make widgets on half power and be run by monkeys') is taken for a laugh and not put down as evidence for the prosecution whose clients have hired monkeys and tried to work through power cuts! Hence, under pressure, do not overcommit yourself, or oversell your wonderful product.

Everything takes time and sometimes even longer

The problems of Soviet performance negotiations are compounded by their 'on-off' nature. The Soviet Union does not run its affairs to suit your timetables; the engineering inspectors from the State Committee that you met last month do not rush back to their offices and immediately send a fully worked through report on their negotiations to their superiors, and neither does it occur to the next layer of specialists – perhaps from the region where the plant that is going to use your product is sited – to immediately jump on a train or plane and come and see you, just because you are twiddling your thumbs in the Hotel Ukraine, in Moscow.

Bureaucrats, especially those in communist countries, are subject to multifarious pressures from above and below their niche in the structure they work in, and it is most unlikely that your timetable features very high on their list of priorities (which generally include keeping their heads down and out of controversy, given the drab alternatives for them if they screw things up).

They will get round to you and your negotiations about as fast as the notoriously slow Soviet waiters get round their restaurants – indeed, even Soviet waiters can seem like greased lightning compared to some of the Kafka-like bureaucrats you have to deal with (unless, of course, you are a supplier of something somebody way up the structure happens to want badly, in which case they might stir themselves – but not a great deal). It has been joked that the Russian language does not include a word with quite the precise sense of urgency implied by *mañana*!

There is little point you sending letters and telexes during the negotiations, asking them what is happening. You won't find out much this way, so save your postage and wait, for it takes longer to get approval to send a letter (evidence!) to the West on what is going on – mainly because they are unlikely to know themselves – than it does to let the decision process grind on regardless. If you really need to do business with the Soviets very badly you have certainly chosen the wrong market in which to get quick results.

Price negotiations

Price negotiations with communist bureaucrats have special features. Not the least is the capacity of the average Soviet official to drive a hard bargain. Two generations of communism have not yet knocked out of Soviet citizens a basic instinct for trading.

You are not dealing with guys who trade their assets for beads and broken mirrors. They may not know the true accounting cost of any of their economy's products, having adopted an accounting system devised by Stalin who had a management style unaccountable to anybody, but they sure know the age old trading principle of offering a little for a lot.

Their capacity as traders, allied to their political prejudices against the filthy rich capitalists who are trying to rip them off, forces them to put pressure on Western quoted prices – no matter how low or profitless your opening prices may be to you. They do not believe you when you put up trimmed prices in the negotiations – they will not accept your first price under any circumstance, so you had better build in a negotiating margin from the start and fight to hold it to the bitter end.

You have two strategies: start with your list prices (a copy of which they require as part of their documentation – though you could have a special one printed for them with all your prices upped by an appropriate premium to give you negotiating room later) and hold a slide below them to as small a discount as possible; or, start openly with a premium (say, 15 per cent) above your list prices on the grounds that trading with communist economies is fraught with additional risks and expense to you.

The first strategy is, in my view, a poor one (only partly rescued by the deception of a separate Soviet price list). Of course, your Soviet official has dreamt up some plausible sounding arguments to tempt you to adopt it. The most frequent is his claim that, as he represents a monopoly trading organization, you need only sell once to him and this must keep your marketing costs down, which should be reflected in lower prices.

Comparable marketing costs in capitalist economies have to include several selling operations with each individual customer, and, hence, the Soviet official is not misleading you, except in respect of the time it takes to complete a full cycle of negotiations with him – two years is not an infrequent investment of your time (and expense) for comradely negotiations.

The second strategy is preferable (and must appeal to the negotiator in you, otherwise you're reading the wrong book). You should bear in mind that exporting your products involves additional costs to you over and above those of getting your products to your factory gate.

Sending negotiators on trips abroad costs cash, so does funding staff time for negotiating with overseas clients, sending out samples, exhibiting at fairs, promotion and advertising, corresponding, telephoning and telexing with customers, waiting for on-site inspection reports and negotiating consequential action from the same, meeting special packing requirements, shipping the products to the ports (FOB) or to the customer (CIF), allowing for returns or breakdowns and putting the problem right, perhaps with your own engineers sent out as troubleshooters, and managing a service organization for the overseas buyer.

There is no reason (other than your gullibility) why you should absolve the Soviet buyer of the additional costs that arise as a direct result of serving him, or any other overseas customer. You are not gilding the lily by seeking to cover your real costs of doing business with his country; you are merely arranging to stay in business in your own!

You will help yourself achieve the latter by watching the commitment to a fixed price at the start of your negotiations. Months, maybe years, later, those fixed prices will look suicidal to your accountants, and that is before the contract is finally signed. By the time deliveries are completed your fixed prices will be positively kamikaze. You can avoid such disasters by quoting prices 'good for ninety days' in your initial bid for the business, and allowing for them to be revised upwards in line with Western inflation rates for the duration of the contract.

Soviet negotiators do not know much about inflation – all prices in communist economies are fixed by the state and don't change unless the state wants them to (so, instead of inflation, they have

DOING BUSINESS WITH IVAN COSTS YOU

The Soviet system for conducting foreign trade starts from the interests of the Soviet state and not the financial health of those eager to trade with them.

In order to tempt you into cutting your prices they will try the 'sell cheap, get famous' gambit: 'low prices on this first order will lead to additional business in later years' they will tell you. The truth is: it won't! Under no circumstances trim your prices for future Soviet trade. As soon as they get a low price they will expect, nay, demand, that they remain low for ever.

Communist negotiators know all about intimidation (their political system is based on it) and they will try to intimidate you with some of the oldest buyer's gambits in the history of negotiating. Among these, there is, of course, 'Noah's Ark' (it's been around that long!): 'We cannot do business with you because your prices are too high compared to the prices of your competitors with whom we are at this moment about to sign a deal.'

In some versions of Noah's Ark they actually shout loudly, bang the table and even stage a walk-out! Your best response? Unflappability. Why? *It's always a bluff.* If they did have lower prices from the competition they would have no reason to talk to you. If you cut your prices on the basis of this performance, you are going to regret it.

Remember: it costs more to do business with the Soviets because you have to invest considerable resources, including executive time, in setting up the deal, probably over several years; you might be faced with heavy penalty payments – which you can bet a rouble to a kopek they will collect on; it will cost you more to get insurance cover and financial aid for your transactions with the Soviets; and they expect your prices to remain stable irrespective of inflation; and if interest rates are involved on the credits you provide to them for their purchases, they have a fixed interest rate of 6 per cent applied to all of their business, irrespective of what it costs you in the West to borrow money. Hence, pad, don't strip, your quoted prices and hang on to them tenaciously.

shortages of goods and long queues for those that they have) and, therefore, they will resist a price inflater clause in the contract. On the other hand, they want your goods and it is best that your negotiating stance requires them to learn to adjust to the phenomenon of Western inflation rather than requiring that you adjust to their 'non-inflationary' accounting system by following a kamikaze fixed price policy.

Another cost that you must consider is that of the agent, if you are using one. Agency commission is usually a percentage (straight or sliding) of the gross sale value and this either comes out of your profits (oh dear!) or is treated as a selling cost and added as a mark-up to your prices (always a sound thing to do!).

Barter deals

Soviet price negotiations can be complicated by the preference for barter-only or part-barter deals among communist foreign trade organizations. Their incentive to try for these non-cash deals is quite simple: they don't have a lot of 'hard' cash that is suitable for foreign trade; the paper money they do have (the rouble) is of such international value that nobody outside a funny farm is likely to want it for other than wallpaper (it is also illegal to import or export roubles across a Soviet frontier – so beware!).

The demand for a barter deal is part of the negotiation on price, for, having tied you up in prolonged negotiations that have switched your 'got-a-deal' euphoria on and off like a Blackpool illumination, and having driven hard against your dollar price, they will introduce the demand to pay some, or even all (if they have your measure), of the cost of your products in the form of goods from a list they provide you with (and they will try damn hard to keep the number of items on that list as small as possible).

Faced with this obstacle, and fearing to lose a deal that you have already invested much time and trouble in keeping alive for two years, you are under a lot of pressure to carry on and accept this twist in your fate. They know this, which is why they save this move until the precise moment when the pressure of your past investment is at its greatest.

Instead of getting $300,000 in cash, you could be faced with a demand (complete with bureaucratic theatricals out of the Eisenstein School of Dramatic Art) that you take half of it in candlewax or Rubic cubes.

You may be lucky and get a bargain, though don't bet on it. If what they offer could be sold easily for hard currency they would have tried that before they offered it to you, unless it's one of those bureaucratic cock-ups that they are sometimes famous for, in which case you might end up grinning like a clown from the Russian State Circus when you sell on their barter goods to a delighted Western customer.

In some deals, particularly in the chemical processing industry, part payment may be offered from the output of the plant that you are supplying. In some commodity markets this can be acceptable, provided you are sure of the quality of the output or that it is of a composition usable in Western or third-party markets, and that you pay attention in the negotiations to the add-on costs of getting it out of the Soviet Union to where you can store, part-process or sell it on. A million barrels of petroleum crude in Omsk is a different proposition to the same cargo delivered alongside a Thames refinery.

The Soviet negotiators could assert that they can only finance your deal if you take barter goods or help them arrange the sale of some goods to a third party for hard currency. Time, risk and expense must enter your mind when this is proposed. But watch it, as their next move could indicate that the barter demand was a double bluff to get you to seek to avoid the expenses of barter by offering them a discount off the cash price you have quoted!

These Russians are *not*, repeat NOT, anybody's fools when it comes to negotiating ploys and gambits – if you stay off the vodka and watch carefully, they might teach you something about how to do business, and lead you to be grateful that they are not competing with us as capitalists.

Answers to self-assessment test 3

1 (a) Not at a preliminary meeting. They will concentrate on technical specifications first. However, if you are price-conscious you will always invite a price objection. (-5)

   (b) Yes. They will trawl over your technical specifications with great care, so be ready for this. (10)

   (c) Not at first. The Soviet economic system is not·very efficient but once you commit yourself to a delivery date you had better keep it or face a penalty charge. (-5) *(d)* Soviet negotiators take a great (even obsessive) interest in performance standards, but you should know what your products can do and hence this ought not to be a problem.

(-7)

(e) Export licences can prove to be a big problem, given the prohibition in the West of exporting products that can have military applications. Make sure that your deal is conditional on you getting an export licence.   (3)

(f) Could be a problem at the end of the negotiation and will require both firmness and imagination on your part. Pad your prices beforehand otherwise you might make a loss.

(5)

2 *(a)* Almost impossible to develop a personal relationship with a Soviet negotiator and not very wise anyway.   (-10)

(b) By far the best policy. Show respect but do not get too involved.   (10)

3 *(a)* Soviet negotiators often try to intimidate you to drop your price because of alleged competition. Resist this ploy. If you are a price-crumbler you should stay at home.   (-10)

(b) You are a price-crumbler!   (-10)

(c) No! That is why they try to pressurize you with the alleged competition.   (-10)

(d) Yes! Alleged competition is *never* a reason for moving on your prices.   (10)

TIPS FOR TRAVELLERS IN SOVIET TERRITORIES

When in conversation with negotiators of Eastern European communist states do not introduce the topic of the Soviet Union; best leave it alone. You may be talking to a dedicated Russophile, on the other hand you may not be, and whether or not they are dedicated communists need have nothing to do with their attitude to the Russians!

Do not carry with you anything that can be remotely connected with politics, including recent issues of any Western newspaper (unless it is the communist *Morning Star*, *L'Unita,* or *L'Humanité*). Take particular care to have no books, especially those written by Soviet dissidents or detractors, that might be regarded as critical of the 'socialist achievements' of the East. You should also avoid carrying religious tracts, more than one copy of the Bible, and certainly nothing about Israel.

Entrepreneurs among you must forgo the regular opportunities to make private deals with nationals of these countries, particularly in respect of foreign currency, but also including Western style clothes and personal effects. Strictly a high risk business, with severe punishments if caught (hence, the attractive rates you will be offered), and it should be avoided, politely but firmly, on all occasions.

The situation regarding bath plugs is improving (why there is a shortage is a mystery). Travel prepared and take with you a larger sized golf ball. Some toilet facilities may strike you as primitive, especially the stand and squat variety. The staff in the hotels used by foreigners are immovable from their routines; the women at the end of each corridor watch all arrivals at and departures from the bedrooms and never sleep; and the slothful service in the state retail organization, GUM, suggests it should be renamed GLUM.

Taxi drivers, hotel porters, and waiters (but *not* frontier guards, policemen, and officials) expect to be tipped. Small inexpensive presents – a company pen, a miniature bottle of

Scotch, a picture postcard of your works, town or memorial, a bunch of flowers – are permissible. You will be inundated with tin badges, flowers and notepads. You may be surprised just how many ordinary people speak English.

If offered a sexual encounter, resist the temptation. It is not unknown for foreigners to be blackmailed for their company's secrets. Also, watch who you drink with – your drink may be drugged as a prelude to sexual blackmail.

Be moderate in your drinking too. Formal lunches in company premises can involve several 'toasts' (to 'mutual friendship between your countries', to 'world peace', to 'the women of the world', to 'the children of the world', to 'peaceful coexistence', to 'the dead of the Great Patriotic War', to 'the President of the USSR and the Prime Minister of Britain', to 'International knitting machinists' day', and so on) and you are expected to swallow the alcoholic, usually neat vodka, contents of your glass in one go, ready for it to be filled up to the brim for the next toast. Get smart, beat them to it, and keep your glass filled with mineral water or lemonade which is always provided on the table.

All appointments with communist officials and negotiators should be fulfilled punctually. They do not like to be kept waiting. Appointments can take some time to arrange. So can visas. It is said that the real reason why Soviet spy, Kim Philby, hung around Beirut while waiting to flee to Moscow, was because it took that long for his visa to come through!

There is little in the way of Western entertainment but most of the communist countries have excellent museums and historic buildings to visit, and well worth it they are too. You will not find much in the world to beat Leningrad's Hermitage. There is a strong emphasis everywhere on official state politics – posters, statues, banners and hoardings show endless effigies of Marx, Engels and Lenin and countless slogans. The Great Patriotic War (World War II) is remembered everywhere. Keep out of trouble by showing respect – remember what you are there for.

Self-assessment test 4

1 You are in Kobe, Japan, discussing the possibility of business with a local company and the leader of the Japanese team hands you a colourfully wrapped box which is clearly intended as a personal gift. Do you:
   (a) Thank him profusely and open the box?
   (b) Thank him profusely and put the box away?
   (c) Thank him profusely and hand him a gift in return?

2 On arrival at Narita airport, Tokyo, you are met by your Japanese hosts, who kindly enquire as to your return journey, offering to check your reservations for you and to handle any related matters during your stay. Do you regard this as:
   (a) An example of Japanese courtesy?
   (b) A means of finding out your time deadlines?

3 When you are considering doing business with a Japanese company, which of the following would you and they consider to be the most important?
   (a) The profitability of your company?
   (b) Its market share?
   (c) Its growth rate?
   (d) Its labour relations?

5 The land of the rising yen
or, where not to take yes for an answer

Change and continuity

Japan is different. It is also rapidly growing into the world's largest national economy. At present it is the second largest industrial power – the United States is the largest and will remain so for much of the rest of the twentieth century, but beyond that it is more likely that Japan will become number one (*dai-chi!*).

Unlike the United States, which relies on only ten per cent of its multi-trillion dollar economy for international trade, with the Japanese, the proportion is more like 30 per cent. That means it is, and will remain, in the business of trading worldwide for its living. In turn, this means that it is more than likely that your own business interests are going to be influenced, directly or indirectly, by the Japanese. Either you will buy or sell with them – in which case you had better get your act together as a negotiator – or you will buy or sell in competition with them – in which case you had better get your act even more together!

The Japanese are unique because of the way they have handled the transition from a traditional and ancient society to a bustling and modern one. In many ways they are a 'model' for those who would also wish to combine change with maintaining traditional values and mores more or less as they have been for centuries. Much of the unrest faced by the late Shah of Iran was caused by the clash between tradition and change (the old ways versus modernization), and, it is said, if there is ever going to be real trouble in Saudi Arabia it will arise from the conflicting values of purist Islam in confrontation with the sin of progress.

Japan's process of change began with the Meiji restoration in 1868 and, by excelling in modernization without overturning its traditional values, it has continued until the country is on the brink of overtaking the USA.

The role of courtesy

To do business with the Japanese you must make some effort to understand how they function (better still, if you have the time, you should try to appreciate *why* they function the way that they do). The shortest way to express what I mean here is to say that for the Japanese everything is managed by a strict routine of courtesy.

Courtesy is more than just being polite. In a traditional society courtesy expresses the role everybody has in the 'proper' (that is, traditional) order of things. People interact within their own group and their manners express mutual recognition of their membership of the group. People also interact outside their own group with people in other groups, and courtesy here enables them to interact in mutual recognition of each other's group role.

Hence, members of the family behave in a certain way with each other, and they behave in a certain way with members of other families. Courtesy facilitates contact between individuals in a way that does not threaten the established order, whether it be the family, the company, the government or whatever.

As a Westerner, you will have extended to you the courtesies of the group or groups to which you are properly introduced and admitted. From the moment that you hand over your own business card and find it studied by your Japanese contact – who will have handed his over in the same expectation – you will be drawn into a social system without parallel in the West.

How rapidly you build up your rapport with your Japanese opposite number will determine whether and to what extent you will do business. You cannot overestimate the role of mutual respect, friendliness and rapport in your relations with the Japanese.

Much of what passes for quaint custom and ritual in Japan is actually an expression of their need to peruse you and your company (and its propositions) for signs that there is a potential for long and fruitful business based on strong and enduring personal relationships.

If you are in a hurry, or do not consider personal relationships of any value, or cannot abide messing about with highly polite (and, to most Westerners, almost excessively polite) exchanges of conversation, gifts and kindnesses, or, to the Japanese mind, are quite rude, you are unlikely to secure much interest in what you have come to sell (or buy).

CARDS PLEASE!

The exchange of business cards in Japan is an absolutely essential ritual, so you must go prepared with several hundred cards, preferably printed on one side in English and the other in Japanese.

Do not underestimate the social requirement for exchanging your card with *everybody* that you meet. This includes offering and receiving one card for every person in the room – even if there are twenty people at the meeting on both sides!

A British negotiator once exchanged 112 business cards at the start of a session. It took fifteen minutes to complete the ritual and he knew that there was no way honour and mutual respect could be satisfied until he had been round the entire room to each person to exchange a bow and a card. He also made sure that he looked carefully at the cards he was offered even though many of them were in Japanese without English translations.

Japanese use of time

The role of time in negotiating with the Japanese can easily be misunderstood (I certainly misunderstood it for some years until I got more familiar with the Japanese mode of business). For example, in *Everything is Negotiable!* (1982) I drew the reader's attention to the potential weakness that a deadline can impose on a Western negotiator. I did this by asking a self-assessment question similar to question 2 at the head of this chapter. The question derives from the experience of several negotiators who on their arrival in Japan are met by their contacts and go through the ritual of having their air-ticket reservations scrutinized, ostensibly, I suggested, in the interests of extending a service but really with another motivation.

I implied in my earlier book that the real purpose behind this move was for the Japanese to discover the deadline towards which the Western negotiator will be working, in order, I asserted, to use this information to apply pressure and secure concessions.

The truth is slightly more complicated (though with some Japanese my original implication may have some foundation). Time is needed by the Japanese to consider all the implications of a business proposal and they carry out this consultation much more thoroughly than is common in Europe or the United States.

The Japanese process of consultation (*ringi-seido*) could bring to the surface problems not appreciated or known to the senior managers negotiating on behalf of the company. This in turn will require further consultations to see what can be done to remove the problems. All of this takes time as the decision passes up and down the company structure.

Meanwhile the Western negotiator will be kept waiting. Nothing he does can hurry up the process, though impatient intervention during it, or signs of disapproval, could slow it down or even make it unnecessary – they could decide that you are showing disrespect and are not the sort of person with whom they want to do any business.

In part, my earlier view was based on discussions with other negotiators to whom the incident had happened and from which they derived the conclusions alluded to in my answer to the self-assessment question. From additional experience I now see that these conclusions were in error, or at least not entirely the complete picture.

Let me explain. There is no doubt that Western negotiators operate at a different pace to their Japanese counterparts. This reflects the differing decision-making systems common to well-managed companies in both cultures. The Japanese take what seems to be an inordinate amount of time to reach a decision. This is because their management system requires that a full consultation takes place with all persons in the organization who are likely to be influenced by the decision.

It is the need to get into mutual balance that distinguishes the Japanese businessman in his contact with non-Japanese negotiators. Only when they feel 'on the same wavelength' will they begin their business and all that precedes this stage is aimed at achieving an interpersonal harmony.

This contrasts with the normal Western approach of sales staff who often make commitments on behalf of their company which are not necessarily confirmed beforehand by their production counterparts. As we all know, sales staff can and do promise potential clients almost anything to get the order, including performance levels, quantities and delivery dates that are not possible in practice. This causes the familiar tension between sales and production (and between sales and accounts – the former

SUMO WRESTLING AND NEGOTIATING

The Japanese can spend what appears to Westerners to be an unprecedented amount of time in preliminaries before discussing their business. These preliminaries have, however, an essential role to play and cannot be skipped through, if you want to get the best deal that is available.

An international banker, with many years' experience of negotiating with the Japanese on joint US-Japanese ventures, explains it as follows:

Negotiating with the Japanese goes through several phases, of which the first is probably the most crucial (for the other phases, in the main, follow internationally recognized norms).

The opening phase is like two Sumo wrestlers facing each other before the start of their contest. They make highly ritualized and absolutely expected genuflections, and go through a detailed ritual involving salt being thrown in each corner and much bowing and other demonstrations of respect.

Then they engage each other's attention and prepare themselves. They examine each other and pace their breathing, gradually increasing the tempo until they are both sure that they are ready. Then, and only then, do they lunge forward.

Neither will move towards the other until they are absolutely sure that they are in balance with each other, both physically and mentally.

preferring that the company holds vast stocks of everything in all variations just in case a customer wants to buy one, and the latter preferring that the company has no stocks at all because stocks tie up capital, etc.).

A well-managed Japanese company (and not all Japanese companies are well-managed) will require that a commitment offered to another company is endorsed by those whose actions will determine in practice if that commitment is to be met.

Failure to meet a commitment is a serious matter and the Japanese prefer to take time out before they make a commitment to make sure that everybody (and I mean everybody) in the organization understands the commitment and agrees to it being

JADE POT BLAMES RED KETTLE

A Japanese negotiating team met their match when they spent many fruitless months trying to negotiate a business deal with the Soviet Union. They specialized in heavy machinery for open cast mineral extraction and the Soviet government wanted to acquire their technology for use in Siberia.

The negotiating teams from the two cultures did not get on at all well. In fact, negotiations got bogged down and the Japanese returned home more than a little demoralized at their experiences.

First, the Japanese complained that their opposite numbers on the Soviet team were quite uninterested in developing personal relationships and rebuffed all Japanese attempts at conviviality. Moreover, the Soviet team changed personnel several times during the six months the Japanese were in Prestoplavsk.

Second, the Soviets took an excessively long time to make a decision, which will cause a wry smile among those who negotiate with Japanese companies and indicate just how long the Soviets must have been taking if it was so long that the Japanese felt they had cause to complain about it!

Third, the Japanese felt that the Soviets, because of their monopoly position as the sole customer for Japanese products in Siberia, were using unfair tactics by having several Japanese companies competing for the same business and by keeping them apart from each other in case they compared notes.

Fourth, the Japanese were appalled at the amount of detail the Soviet negotiators wanted (implying that the Japanese were not capable of producing world-class machinery) and they were apprehensive at the extent of the proposed contract that the Soviets wanted the Japanese to sign (implying a lack of trust in Japanese commitments).

Lastly, the Japanese complained that Prestoplavsk was an awful place to spend much time in and that their Soviet 'hosts' left them to their own devices for social entertainment, often for days on end. Also, they only got decisions to go ahead on important details just as the Japanese had to leave to get transport home.

given, rather than that they be forced to spend time later on trying to sort out what to do about a commitment that should not have been given in the first place, and have to chastise those who have failed in some way to honour the commitment given in the company's name.

If a delivery date is being given, then clearly those parts of the company responsible for designing, constructing and completing the product will have to be consulted to see if they can meet that date. A Japanese company requires a formal written endorsement from each manager responsible for each activity and will expect each manager to have consulted his workforce before he gives his endorsement.

When a Western company overextends itself this creates problems for those whose job is made more difficult as a consequence. The usual message from the top of a Western company that has overextended itself to those who feel overwhelmed in consequence of this situation is often a single instruction: 'Cope!'. A Japanese company avoids this situation by in-depth consultation and agreement beforehand. But detailed consultation takes time. The Japanese regard this as time well spent. So should you.

Westerners' perceptions of their own deadlines
From the point of view of an uninformed negotiator who makes a short visit to Japan in order to sign an agreement, the details of which he plans to negotiate face-to-face with his Japanese contacts, the delays in getting a decision look quite different. We always assume the worst when we contemplate the source of our inconvenience.

You assume that the delay is aimed at putting on negotiating pressure as your deadline to return home approaches. 'Did they not make a point of enquiring when I had to leave?' 'Is it not the case that we have spent several weeks in socializing, with short bursts of negotiating activity lasting a day or so, and now, just as I have two days left before departing, are they not presenting me with amended proposals?'

The answers convince you that you are dealing with tactics aimed at using your deadlines to pressurize you into making concessions. When you add to your suspicions the fact that you did make concessions in those last hurried meetings before walking on to your

57

WHO'S BOTHERED ABOUT PENALTIES?

A British shipping company required to replace some of its bulk carriers and opened negotiations with British Shipbuilders and some Japanese yards before placing their order. Negotiations with British Shipbuilders took the normal route of hard bargaining on prices and just as hard bargaining on the size of the penalty payments for (the expected) late delivery. They felt they got a good deal here when British Shipbuilders offered a £2 million penalty for late delivery.

The Japanese matched the British prices for building the ships and promised as good a delivery date. When it came to the penalty price for late delivery, the Japanese invited the British to write in the contract 'any sum you like, we will not argue over the amount'. This caught the British negotiators by surprise and they asked if the Japanese were serious, expecting a long argument about delivery penalties.

'Of course we are serious' the Japanese insisted. 'Fill in the total price of the ship if you like.'

This told the British, beyond any doubt, that the Japanese were certain to meet their delivery promises, in contrast to the long haggles they had experienced with British Shipbuilders.

The orders went to the Japanese yard.

departing aircraft, you complete your belief in the scenario that deadline hustling is a peculiarly Japanese tactic.

It might look that way but it almost certainly is not (though no one can blame the Japanese if they accept the concessions offered to them by a time-pressurized Western negotiator). Delays during a negotiation are a consequence of a necessary part of their management system. The amended proposals they present to you on their return to the negotiations will have arisen out of their consultations and represent the concensus of their management team. The fact that you are now in a hurry to return from whence you came is not their fault; their earlier interest in your departure deadline is purely one of ascertaining what time they have available for doing business with you.

The counter to deadline pressure – from whatever source you experience it – is, of course, not to have deadlines in the first place.

If you go to Japan to do business in a hurry it is your sense of time that is wrong, not theirs. If you went to Japan with an intention of spending a month or more, thus giving them time to consult their people, you would not be under the self-inflicted pressure of your own deadlines. There is nothing to stop you taking longer time to conduct your business with the Japanese (if there is, then perhaps you should try selling to the US of A rather than to Japan). You can just as easily visit them and leave your proposals on the table while they think about them and arrange to get their own management's agreement. You can always use the time available to visit other companies or other parts of the same company, or you can return in a month or two when they are ready to reply with their considered response.

If you insist on everything being settled in a week or ten days you are going to be as disappointed as you are suspicious. Hence, the time pressure that many Western negotiators feel they are the victims of is just as often the result of their own attempt to pressurize the Japanese into an earlier settlement than they are ready for. Think of your behaviour from their point of view: why is this person in such a hurry? Is there something in his proposals that we have not noticed, perhaps we should re-examine them?

International negotiators have to accept that the pace of a negotiation will always be determined by the pace of the dominant party. If this is clearly understood by the negotiator visiting Japan it will produce a lot of respect from the Japanese, and, in Japan, business goes to those whom the other party respects the most.

The quest for technical details

Like the Soviets, the Japanese are avaricious when it comes to acquiring technical details of your products, though the motivation in the Japanese's case is somewhat more honourable. The Soviet negotiator seeks to protect himself from accepting something that is not quite kosher and at the same time engages in some *en passant* technological 'espionage'. The Japanese are more likely to be establishing through their technical queries the technical soundness of the product and your own suitability as a person with whom to entrust their business future.

If they are going to acquire a licence to manufacture your product, they must, of course, know everything there is to know about your product. Likewise, if they are going to act as agents in Japan to sell your product, at the very least their own sales agents and service people will need to know everything they can about your product.

The meetings that take place between your team and theirs in Japan will involve considerable portions of time spent interrogating (there is no other word for it) you and your team, and not just on the technical qualities of what you produce. They will expect you to know the finest details of the financial arrangements of your business, including market share, growth rates and the intricacies of your company's place in the wider context of the industry you are in and, where applicable, in your company's structure if you are a subsidiary of a larger organization.

Profits or growth?
Western business negotiators tend to be more concerned with profitability than with growth rates. The difference is interesting, though its basis is not entirely a cultural one. It reflects the entrepreneurial psychology more common in expanding Japan than in the more recession-obsessed West. Several Western entrepreneurs are more 'Japanese' in their attitudes to growth than their contemporaries and this suggests that the difference in outlook is not entirely culture based.

The Japanese business leader will study the relative market shares of his own and rival companies in all of the product lines they handle. He will be interested in growth rates of sales and the steady drive to domination in each sector of the market. His judgements about how well a company is managed will be influenced greatly by what he sees in these figures.

Whether a plant is profitable or, more correctly (because some level of profit is required if a business is to be sustained), how profitable the business is, will be of less interest to him, and, indeed, could actually cause him to worry if the profit levels are (by Japanese standards) exceptionally high, for this indicates something is wrong with the sales drive.

The Japanese will always opt for increasing their outlays on sales (both by direct marketing and by aggressive prices) than for accumulating high profit levels. They live their business lives on the edge of constant growth rather than in safe consolidation of previously successful products. The entrepreneurial Western businessman behaves in much the same fashion, with the difference that he is more likely to be an exception in his own country rather than, as in Japan, the rule.

Attitudes to investment

A few very large companies dominate the domestic Japanese market. They also dominate the import business. They rely heavily on bank-financed loans for their operations and their expansion. They do not worry too much about the ratio of debt interest to profits, as long as they are expanding, and to expand they must invest in extending their capacity to produce more.

The contrast with a Western (especially UK business) is stark. A British firm will see investment as a means of reducing labour while maintaining output. This leads to lower unit costs and therefore, at least in theory, to increased or maintained unit profits from doing much as they did the previous year.

A Japanese company will see investment in equipment as a means of expanding output with the same workforce, and regard the job of selling the additional output as a challenge to its philosophy of growth. Nowhere is the consequence of this different approach seen more clearly than in the attitude of the respective labour forces to the role of investment: in the UK, new technology is equated with job losses (and therefore resisted); in Japan new technology is equated with preserving employment (and therefore accepted).

These differences in outlook explain some of the differences in the preparation negotiators in each country will undertake prior to meeting to discuss potential business opportunities. The Western firm will study (assuming it studies anything at all!) the Japanese firm's financial soundness and its profitability. The Japanese firm will study the Western firm's relative position in its markets, its suppliers, its customers, and its organizational connections (if relevant) with associate companies in the holding group.

In early meetings the Japanese will expect the Western negotiators to know in minute detail everything about their company's financial structure and the financial structure of any company (including rivals, suppliers and customers) with which they compete.

When it comes to price negotiations the Japanese will tend towards aggressive price policies that will maximize sales not maximize profits. To get into a market they will expect to take losses and will not bother too much about so doing. This puts a lot of pressure on Western companies that follow a different pricing policy, assuming that they want to do business with or in Japan.

Avoid contract jargon

Another area where there might be a difference in approach, and because of this a danger to good relations and harmony, is in the question of contracts between the parties. The Japanese are at the other end of the spectrum in the matter of contracts to the Soviets, who normally require the most detailed specification of mutual obligations, including penalty clauses, incorporated into the contract before agreement is reached. With the Japanese the exact opposite tends to be the case.

Business relations with the Japanese are not separated from the mutual respect each party has for the other. In fact, they are an integral part of the same experience. A tightly drawn up contract in the usual legal language common to Western business practice ('party of the first part' and 'party of the second part' etc.) is anathema to the Japanese approach.

First, English legal language is mind-boggling even to the English and, one suspects, few English lawyers fully understand it themselves (they certainly charge enough for giving conflicting interpretations of the same document!). This presents an enormous problem when translated into Japanese (it's bad enough trying to translate an English contract into plain English).

Second, the implication of a heavily documented legal contract written in formal legal language is that the parties need to cover themselves for every eventuality. Now some eventualities are of a sensitive nature (what happens if they run off with the loot?) and, when presented in a stark way to a Japanese negotiator at the start of what is intended to be a mutually beneficial relationship, you run the risk of causing great offence. If you need to cover yourself against the prospect of them being dishonest, or of them failing to meet their obligations in some way, they are likely to think that you do not trust or respect them.

In short they prefer not to do business with people who do not treat them with respect. What might need to be taken for granted in Europe – the need to avoid 'one truck contracts' (that is, a contract that leaves both parties at the mercies of 'Murphy's Law') – if handled carelessly can be deeply offensive in Japan.

Now this is not an unsurmountable problem. My advice is to keep your legal people at arm's length and to require of them that they explain in straightforward English what their legal mumbo jumbo means in language that can be translated into Japanese with the least chance of causing misunderstanding. Better still, work from a

Japanese contract and add in only what is absolutely necessary.

Japanese businesses do not engage in deliberate malpractices, nor will they cheat those with whom they share their business. You can relax a little more than you normally would.

Nothing I have said here should be interpreted as suggesting that the Japanese do not participate in negotiating a contract. They will do so, and they will insist on being very specific in terms of quality, performance, quantity, delivery and specifications. They will also hold to the terms of the contract, but what they find difficult to accept is a multi-clause contract drawn up in legalistic language that suggests from the start that their intentions are suspect or that the worst must be prepared for or insured against.

Importance of personal relationships

The Japanese hold very strongly to the role of personal relationships in their business dealings. They like to get to know the people with whom they intend to do business and they like to deal with the same people over and over again. Here they are not unlike the Chinese, who reserve a special place in their negotiations for 'old friends' (that is, foreigners they have dealt with before or who are introduced to them by somebody they revere or trust – usually another 'old friend'). Similarly with negotiators in South America. They too like to 'relate' to the people who want to do business with them. If this proves not possible – the 'chemistry' is wrong, for example – it is unlikely that business will be contracted.

The domination of interpersonal relations in the outlook and approach of Japanese negotiators finds its populist expression in the almost total inability of the Japanese to utter the word 'no', even when they wish to do so, and their substitution of a complicated, though unintentional, prevarication when put into a situation where to a Westerner 'no' is the appropriate answer to a question.

Almost being unable to say 'no', they can be misunderstood when they say 'yes' ('Hai!'). If you have asked a question that requires them to say 'no', it is your fault for asking the question in that way if you end up disappointed by their inability to deliver on the 'yes'. (A similar problem is found among the Arabs – saying 'no' implies that they do not want to help, so they say 'yes' even if they have no means of fulfilling that sort of commitment.)

This can be very off-putting when you hear a stream of 'Hai! Hai!' sounds and think he is saying 'yes' to your proposals. He might just be letting you know that he is listening to what you have to say. This leads to the indirect approach in conversation. To tell you that your proposition is unacceptable by saying 'no' would give offence so he will say words to the effect that your proposal 'could be better if it took in this or that'. How many 'this's' or 'thats' would tell you just how unacceptable your proposition was!

Listening for signals from a Japanese negotiator is even more essential than when dealing with your own colleagues. They will try to nudge you towards what they want rather than go at you with a direct proposition, particularly if it contradicts something for which you have expressed a preference or where it could indicate that you have not been paying attention (hence, avoid asking them if they have understood your proposition as they will say 'Hai', even if you were totally incomprehensible!).

In the land of the rising yen (and it will continue to rise for many a year yet) it is best if you are exceptionally polite, completely relaxed about time, and know that you must never take 'yes' for an answer!

Answers to self-assessment test 4

1 *(a)* Always thank your Japanese hosts for anything they do for you, even well beyond the point at which your thanks would be a cause for comment in the UK. But do not open any wrapped gift in these circumstances, unless expressly urged to do so by the person who gave it to you. There is a danger that he or she might lose face by offering to you a gift that is too expensive (compared to the one you intended to give) or too cheap.   (-5)

 (b) Yes. In putting it away do so carefully and tell the person who gave it to you how unworthy you are to receive such generous treatment.   (5)

 (c) Even better. A small gift, neatly wrapped in traditional Japanese design paper and tied with a nice bow is always welcome. The value is less important than the thought. If you were unprepared for the gift exchange ritual, do not panic. A small token at the time, followed by a proper gift at the next opportunity will do fine. In this respect, if your Japanese partner requires something which you promise to send on to him, *do so*, even at the cost of extraordinary effort – it will pay you back many times over.   (10)

2 (a) More than likely. The Japanese are exceptionally polite and go out of their way to help you. It is best to treat this event with an open mind (and, just to make sure that it is a courtesy only, always travel to Japan with open return tickets without a deadline on them!). (5)

(b) They could have this motivation, though much of the problem with Western negotiators is their tendency to try to rush things in Japan and the deadlines that they feel strangled by are often of their own making. (-5)

3 (a) Unlikely to be a decisive consideration. (-5)

(b) Yes. Your market share tells them about your market strengths (or weaknesses). If you are seeking to supply their markets they will expect large volume from you; if you are seeking to represent them in your territory they will want you to do so if you can move large volumes for them. (10)

(c) A high growth rate can compensate for a currently low market share. It will also tell them how entrepreneurial you and your company are and what they can expect from you. (5)

(d) Japanese industrial relations can be stormy. Their interest in your industrial relations would reflect their estimate of your capacity to produce output or provide a service. In Japanese eyes constant strikes over 'trivial' issues suggest that there is something wrong with your management style. (3)

Self-assessment test 5

1 You are arranging to visit a number of Arab countries in order to promote your company's products and to secure local agencies to distribute them in local markets. How many days do you allow for your itinerary which is to include Egypt, Saudi Arabia, Oman, Kuwait, Iraq and Libya?

   (a) 7
   (b) 14
   (c) 18
   (d) 21
   (e) 28
   (f) 31

2 You have been given an interview with a leading local Arab agent and have spent several hours socializing and drinking coffee. No business has been discussed and you are anxious to get the discussion of your proposals under way. Do you:

   (a) Raise the subject in a lull in the conversation?
   (b) Wait until your host raises the matter?

3 You have decided to wait until your host raises the subject, and it is time for you to leave. Do you:

   (a) Ask him when you can return to see him?
   (b) Leave a set of materials about your products?
   (c) Ask him for a definite date for an interview to discuss your business?

6 Negotiating with the Arabs
or, how to take your time

The Islamic family

Whereas with the communists the state is the dominating influence in their business lives, with the Arabs it is the extended family (father, brothers, uncles, in-laws and cousins). Obligations to one's family and friends are not treated lightly; they create, and are created by, mutual expectations of help, assistance, support and succour. Warm-hearted nepotism rules, or at least holds great sway.

Your problem as a foreign negotiator can be summed up simply: you are not related to any Arab family and therefore you are an outsider, a true foreigner in their land. To the extent that you compound your lack of familial ties by being ignorant of Arab customs, manners and outlooks (or, worse, disrespectful of them), you will find it very difficult to make much headway in your business relationships with Arabs.

The Arab nation consists of 160 million people in twenty-two states spread across Northern Africa and the Middle-East, from the Atlantic Ocean to the Gulf of Oman. While there are vast variations in outlook, practice and economic capacity between the Arab states, there are certain unifying forces of their societies that keep the spirit of Arab unity alive, and which occasionally blow a little life into its practical application.

The Arabic language is among the most prominent of the unifying forces in the region. Dialects and accents there may be, but the written language and its classical roots reign supreme from one end of the Arab nation to the other. Those who would hope to do a lot of business with Arabs would do well to learn their language – if only to a rudimentary level. In the meantime, many Arab businessmen speak English (and sometimes French), and have degrees and diplomas from Western universities.

The other main unifying force is Islam, for though Islam is now a religious way of life for many beyond the Arab nation, it remains, for the majority of Arabs, a living memory of their history. It pervades all their social structures, and in many of their states it has a grip on the secular that recognizes no separation of church and state.

Some countries, such as Saudi Arabia, Sudan, or Libya, are more Islamic in their secular laws than others, such as Egypt or Bahrain, though the differences are often more of degree than of kind. The availability of, or punishment for having, booze is a reliable, if crude, guide to the Islamic temperature of a country.

While it is not necessary to convert to Islam to do business, it is sensible for you to learn something about Islam, its history and its creeds, and to treat its modern manifestations with respect.

You must not mock by word or grimace whatever you find unusual in their behaviour and you must make no derogatory, or joking, remarks about their beliefs and customs, especially as much of what passes for knowledge of Islam in Western countries is grotesquely inaccurate.

If it is Ramadan, your Arab host will not be eating or drinking until sunset, and, no matter how hungry or thirsty you are, you should try to avoid both food or tea, unless your host has it brought for you into his *diwan* (a room for receiving guests) and where to refuse might give offence. But even then, acknowledge that you know it is Ramadan for him, and nibble or sip unenthusiastically at it, rather than wolf it down like it was your last supper.

If you are insensitive to this type of situation it might very well *be* your last supper as far as business with him is concerned, in which case you will eat, drink and go home empty-handed.

The open door policy
Negotiations with Arabs can never be divorced from their environment, and it is for this environment that you must be prepared. By environment, I don't just mean that sand will be blown into your every orifice (though that is a distinct possibility up-country), nor that it gets very hot during the day and perishing cold at night. The environment I refer to has more to do with the social environment that influences their behaviour as negotiators.

Take their 'open door' policy, for instance. You may well be deep into discussion with an Arab contractor when some of his friends or family arrive at his office. They certainly will not be kept waiting outside the room but will be invited in for tea and talk. Your negotiations will be suspended until they leave, and they will recontinue only for as long as it takes for some more of his friends to arrive. And so it could go on all during your visit to his office (though there are some signs that the traditional 'open door' policy is being curbed by the more commercially minded of the Arabs).

The Arab will not refuse traditional hospitality to those who come to see him, and he can be diverted for many hours a day by social interruptions. You must accept this, no matter how important you might feel you are and how crucial your timetable is to you. It is not rudeness on his part – quite the contrary, it is simply the continuation of the courtesies of the bedouin desert tradition, every bit as necessary for his functioning as a respected person in his society, as it is for you to turn up to work in your trousers and not your pyjamas.

This open door habit infuriates some Western negotiators. If you show signs of impatience to your host, you will be finished. I know one Harvard law graduate who swore to me he would never return to Egypt, no matter what the fee, because he could not stand having his day prolonged by constant interruptions in his discussions with Arab civil servants, who operate the open door policy within government departments for absolutely anybody, their lowest clerks included, even though they (or, rather their fathers and grandfathers) long ago left the imperatives of desert hospitality behind them.

In one respect I had to concur with his draconian decision: if you can't accept Arab ways, don't waste your time trying to do business with Arabs.

The Arab attitude to time
The Arab attitude to time can give an entirely wrong impression to those brought-up closer to the clock than is probably good for them. Americans are often obsessed with time, while Arabs can appear to be totally devoid of any consciousness of time.

Many Arabs know that time is more important than they or their colleagues acknowledge by their behaviour, and attitudes are gradually changing. No doubt a compromise somewhere between the two extremes would do everybody a little good, but the low value placed on time has environmental roots which cannot be ignored just because it is inconvenient to Western attitudes.

The Arabs are not the only nation to place a low value on time: the Italians, Spanish, Portuguese, Mexicans, among others, are notorious for adherence to the *mañana, mañana* school of decision-making. It reflects the non-urban life-style of a pre-industrial society, and it withers only so fast as the effects of urbanization and industrialization spread through the generations.

Hoping for quick decisions from Arabs can be a frustrating experience. On the other hand, they can make quick decisions on occasion (and deciding not to trust you could be one of them!).

Taking a long time to come to a decision about a proposition may not just be an example of muddle and inefficiency – though this can be a singular explanation in some cases. It might indicate that they are displeased with something in your proposition and that, though they have hinted at what is displeasing them, you have not picked up their signals and have not responded to them positively.

If you feel harassed by what you regard as time-wasting, you certainly will not hear nor note the signals, while, if you slowed down to their pace of doing business, and listened carefully to what they were saying, you would learn to spot the problem, and react by amending your proposition in some way (much the same advice applies to negotiating with the Japanese).

Subtle signals

In a sense, a negotiation with an Arab is partly a consultation with him. If you are doing well in your negotiations, you will hear yourself saying: 'Here is what I was thinking of suggesting, what do you think of it', far more than you will confront him with: 'That's my final offer, take it or leave it'.

If you do not reformulate aspects of a proposition you have put to them, rather than say 'no' to your face they will not make a decision at all. They hope time will allow them to get their way, or will permit the issue to die naturally by neglect.

As you brood over your dilemma – 'Why are they avoiding me?' – you might, just might, go over what they said about your proposition and identify, by luck or by judgement, what the problem is and, in re-presenting the issue, assuming you have got it right this time, you might be surprised by the sudden change in pace as you both move on towards agreement.

If you don't see the problem at all, you will return home, cursing the inefficiency of a nation 'that was still riding around on camels while we were in High School' (as my Harvard friend somewhat impudently put it).

Arabs do not like face-to-face confrontations and quarrels with foreigners. They have a tradition of hospitality and politeness. The door that is open to the cousin or the neighbour is also open to you. You have come a long way to see them, and they respect that, and they will go out of their way to make you welcome, no matter what other urgent business is at hand.

Providing you do not upset them with your arrogance and haughtiness (the two qualities Arab negotiators identify in Westerners – especially, I am sorry to say, in the English, though not, I am glad to confirm, in the Scots – as the ones they find most unacceptable), you will eventually get round to talking about business.

They do not like rushing into business subjects as soon as they meet with you. It is bad manners to do so and they will expect you to talk with them about social and other matters for some time – perhaps fifteen minutes or more on most occasions, sometimes several hours, or, on other special occasions, through several meetings.

Your best guide is to leave to the Arab negotiator the decision of when to talk business, and do not under any circumstance be the first to raise the subject.

This can be very off-putting, especially when you have met the Arab for the first time and, as far as you know, he does not know why you have come to see him. In your mind is the thought that unless you tell him that you are looking for a local agent to market your binoculars and range finders, he might think that you are a tourist just passing through the Gulf on your way to play polo in Delhi.

If you are tempted to raise the matter of business first, in one word, don't!

If the interview is clearly at an end, very politely thank him for his generous hospitality and ask if you can come and see him on another day. He will certainly not refuse to see you again (here the open door works for you!) and you can try again.

The Arab businessman may behave generously to a fault, and sometimes appears to have an other-worldly naïveté about him, but he is not at all as stupid as an ignorant Westerner might think – indeed, there are more Arab graduates of Western universities sitting across the carpet negotiating with Western businessmen than there are Western graduates sitting across the carpet negotiating with Arab businessmen!

By showing that you understand the social mores of the Arab peoples he will be more likely to talk business with you when you meet again. If, however, he is away when you next return to see him, or is in and meets with you but does not discuss business, it suggests either that you must keep trying on another occasion, or he is telling you, without being rude, that he does not want to be an agent for binoculars and range finders (he will have found out why you are in Doha or Bahrain without you knowing about it).

Another word of caution is due here: if he does ask you why you have come to see him, do not start off a sales pitch along the lines of 'the great opportunity I am about to offer you to get rich as an agent for my company's products', which is an OK line in Garry, Indiana or Walthamstow, London, but totally out of place in the Middle East.

It is far better to pitch it along the lines of you wanting his help in a business proposition. He is unlikely to need to get richer and will resent the implication that you think he wants to, but he cannot resist 'helping' someone he has learned to respect.

Local agents
All Arab governments insist that you do business through a local agent, whether you are negotiating with a private business or with a government department. This policy has ensured lucrative careers and incomes to Arab nationals, and siphoned back some of the profits to the lands that generated them. It is a sound and sensible policy, very much in the national interests of the Arab countries.

You will not get far without a good Arab go-between. On a big deal, he can help you make the right contacts in the government and those you will need to get a decision to go ahead with the project. He will speed you through the paperwork (taking 'speed' in a relative sense, of course!), arrange for labour, materials, transport, storage and accommodation, and, most importantly, expedite (less slowly than otherwise!) payments to you for your work.

A good local agent is more than somebody working for you, he is a partner in the venture and should be treated as such. He gets his income from commission (a percentage of the gross value of the deal) and he will expect to be consulted about everything, perhaps far more than you normally disclose to your own employees, including for example, your pricing policy.

Just how you handle this aspect of your relationship could influence greatly the energy with which he represents your interests in negotiations with other Arab nationals and government departments. It may appear that he is not doing a great deal for his commission (and the sum you pay to him can appear horrendous when said slowly, especially in comparison with your own earnings for creating the business), but without him you might find out just how bad Arab agents can be when they don't try very hard.

You will have to negotiate with him first about the level of his commission, and this can range from 4 to 9 per cent. On a multi-million dollar deal he is going to be very rich in no time. Sure, you should still haggle for each percentage, or fraction of a percentage, point that he gets in commission. He will expect you to do so, and might get suspicious if you don't.

You will find him accommodating in a negotiation with him and it will follow the same pace as the deals you will do with him as a partner with other nationals. 'What will you be doing for our money?' is a useful question to keep on the table as you negotiate his commission, as is: 'What other major projects have you been agent for?'.

Finding out what you are getting for your money is always a good idea in any negotiation. If you are not impressed with what is on offer you can lower his expectations of the price he will get for his services or you can increase his commitments in return for what he gets.

Previous experience is another useful line of attack. If he was the go-between for a Japanese steel works or an American downstream processing plant, you can have some assurance that he is worth what he is asking (also you have somewhere to go to check on his performance). If yours is his first big project, this is surely going to be reflected in his commission rate?

The ethics of commission etc.
You should pay for a go-between on a results-only basis. His commission is a percentage of the gross value of the business secured, not a commission on the gross value of the business you sought to get. You will want to ensure that if he does not perform he does not get paid; anything else is for you a kamikaze policy.

You can, if the state of the competition lets you, put his commission as a mark-up on your total cost to the client, and you should remember that the competition's go-between's commission will be a mark-up in their bid. If you can't do this, his commission will come out of your profits.

TIMES CHANGE

In 1958, a French car firm agreed to make an Arab businessman its agent in the Gulf. The Arab had approached them seeking an agency and had persuaded them that he had the acumen and the contacts to make the agency profitable.

The French negotiated an agency deal that required the Arab to pay in advance, every six months, for the cars they were about to ship out to him. They regarded this as a prudent necessity to protect themselves in case the Arab failed to meet his commitments.

The requirement to pay in advance almost busted the Arab, as it meant he had to borrow heavily from a local (foreign) bank who took a jaundiced view of lending large sums, on very little security, to local Arab nationals.

Over the years, however, the agency prospered and the Arab sold a lot of cars at a profit and had a thriving spare parts business in support of the main operation.

After the 1973 oil price hike, when billions of dollars worth of income began to flow into the hands of the Gulf Arabs, the demand for cars rocketed and he stood ready to make a great deal from his agency and his considerable experience in this market.

First, he took on the agency for a German car firm as well as the French one, and then he used the terms the Germans were delighted to offer him, in view of projected sales figures, as a basis for re-negotiating the original deal he had with the French, who had no wish to be cut out of the lucrative Gulf market. He was able to re-negotiate the agency deal to get cars on credit. From this he expanded his agency rapidly.

The shift in market demand meant that the agency agreement, held by the Arab in the lean years, was now worth a lot more to the French car firm than it was to the now very rich Arab businessman.

He also set up his own local bank to manage the financial side of the agency, and cut out the foreign bank that had given him a hard time on credit limits before 1973.

Of course, all this talk of a go-between's commission for securing you the business through his contacts (perhaps somebody from his own extended family) hints at being slightly disreputable. Few people exactly call it bribery but it is close to a very narrow line between ethical and unethical business practices.

Now it is not my objective to moralize about the business ethics of other countries, or of foreigners like ourselves in them. The original purposes of the agency system was to give locals a piece of the action and to smooth the way for two cultures to become friends and do good business together. That original purpose is still present, and is enshrined in the commercial laws of many Arab states, but like everything else it can get corrupted if it gets out of hand.

Is it a bribe to hire somebody on a performance contract to help you negotiate a deal with a government department and to help you to supply what you have contracted to do if the deal is signed?

It is a very delicate legal question. If the agent induces somebody else, for a reward (a cut out of his commission, say), to *corruptly* offer the business to his client (i.e. you), it seems to me that this is close to bribery by him of a third party if the only reason that you got the business was the financial inducement that your agent offered. But are you corrupt in this transaction? Not if you are unaware of what your agent did. As far as you are concerned you paid the agent to help you to secure the business; what he does out of sight and without your knowledge or instigation is not something you can be hauled up for – at least not in theory!

Not all Western courts (and not all Arab courts either) have taken this view of those instances that have come to light (the Lockheed scandals, or the Italian oil deals, for example). It is an offence in Europe to corruptly offer inducements to decision-makers to favour you with business.

In so far as your agent is not an officer of a decision-making structure – he is not a civil servant, or officer of a purchasing company, for instance – he is not being bribed by you to secure business.

If, however, he is a decision-maker, or, with your knowledge, is spreading his commission about to corrupt decision-makers, then it is likely that you are engaged in corrupt practices.

How you handle a delicate situation like this, where you suspect you are implicated, innocently or otherwise, with bribery, is, of course, your own affair, and not mine.

As long as you are clear in your own mind that you are paying a commission to a go-between for getting you to the negotiating carpet with Arab decision-makers and are not paying him anything for going between you and the decision-makers with a bag full of dollars, then you ought to be confident that your behaviour will be of no interest to the courts. You can never be sure, though, that you are safe if you are operating in this rather murky area. Arab courts, for example, have not always been neutral or understanding when even senior figures have been charged with straying into bribery: President Sadat's brother was sent to jail for crossing the line between commission and bribery, and so have several Western businessmen in Libya, Iraq, Iran, and Syria.

The worst thing you can say about your Arab go-between, even if he is half decent at his job, is that he takes a long time to do it. On the surface this looks to be a sign of inefficiency – of which you will no doubt get lots of other examples while you stay in hotels or travel about Arab countries.

On the other hand, it may be that you are pacing the deal too fast for the local community. He will spend not a little time socializing while engaged on your behalf in business with other Arabs. The delays that appear to be inflicted upon you will be inflicted upon him, with the difference that he will not be so acutely embarrassed by them as you might be.

The people he deals with have a different set of values from you. For instance, they will regard efficiency with less awe than you do, perhaps considering that loyalty from and to their Arab staff is more important.

Again, psychologically, the Arab is out in the desert, alone with the people upon whom he depends for his very life. Loyalty when there is a water shortage is more important than efficiency – if you doubt this then you have never depended absolutely upon anybody for much that mattered.

The *bedu* is loyal and he is learning about efficiency rather than practising it. You should remember this in your dealing with your agent – show loyalty to him and you will get it back in trumps.

Alleged fatalism

Another carry-over from this earlier age (not all that long past – thirty years ago the bedouin knew the true worth of a camel), is the sense of fatalism. This is a direct consequence of living on the edge of survival where not much changes in the life style of successive

NO AGENTS HERE!

Not all Arab countries insist on a foreign firm having an agent. In Iraq, for example, the government has decided on a deliberate policy of discouraging foreigners from dealing with government agencies through agents. The reasons have much to do with the proclivity that the agent system has for encouraging corruption and the abuse of influence. Also, under socialist influences, the role of agents in enriching themselves runs counter to prevailing ethical standards, even if they are acting as honest go-betweens and in no way corrupting anybody (in Egypt the government encourages agents but requires them to disclose their commission earnings and prohibits them being paid in accounts kept overseas).

It is an offence to use the services of an agent who is not formally registered with the public authorities. To do so risks being black-listed by the government from future business with Iraq. Moreover, even registered agents can be refused access to negotiations on your behalf in some state agencies.

In this atmosphere it is best to avoid dealing with anybody who claims to be able to place a contract your way because of their alleged influence with somebody in the government service. You are unlikely to be given a contract as a result of such a person's activities and are more likely to end up with yourself, or officers from your company, in a local (unpleasant) jail.

In Saudi Arabia, in contrast, while local agents must register with the Ministry of Commerce, their role in acting as intermediaries between the Saudi purchasers (government or private) and the foreign supplier is directly encouraged. But care is needed in selecting an agent in most Arab countries, for once an agreement has been reached with a local national it is extremely difficult to disengage from an agency relationship that has proven to be less than satisfactory (the local courts are not models of objectivity in disputes between locals and foreigners).

generations. The cycle of life is not often interrupted by anything that man does – nature holds dictatorial sway.

The rural societies of those who live close to nature tend to have a fatalistic view of the universe. 'God wills' is an acknowledgement of man's weakness before the natural order of things. Once science is allied to man's needs, nature submits and with it the idea of fatalism.

When Westerners witness Arabs in a fatalistic mood they conclude that this is an essential characteristic of the Arab outlook on life. It is not, and a moment's reflection on the rural societies of Europe in previous centuries, or the indigenous societies of North America, would show this 'fatalism' to be on a par with the superstition and myth of our own pasts (how many Westerners read their 'stars' each day?).

The modern Arab – the one you are likely to be negotiating with – is unlikely to leave his share of the deal to fate! You may take it for granted he will work for the best deal for himself and leave nothing at all to chance.

Arab women

The more perceptive reader will have noticed that this entire chapter has been written in the male gender, as if the female did not exist. This might have antagonized feminists. It has been, however, a deliberate policy on my part to exclude from this chapter any reference until now to Arab women.

It is not that the Arab woman does not count; of course she does in her society. But unless you are mixing business with cultural reform (a short-term activity in the Middle East), the position, and the future, of Arab women is, to be pretty blunt about it, none of your damn business!

Old hands in the Middle East always advise outsiders to steer well clear of even the notion of Arab women while visiting Arab countries. And they do so, for good reason. Arabs do not like interference in their private affairs by foreigners, especially those who know little of what they are talking about.

If you want to join the League for Stirring Up Trouble in Arab Countries, you may go ahead and state your views to whosoever will listen to you. You will not, however, be able to combine such activity with doing business with Arabs.

I was once saved at a dinner party in London from an indiscretion in talking about the subject of Arab women in their homelands. My guests were an Egyptian Arab and his wife, and during the evening I raised the subject of the Arab attitude to women in conversation.

The reply I got came not from the man but from his wife, an articulate educated woman, who spoke better English than I did Arabic, and who knew both Western and Arab societies from having lived in both since she was a schoolgirl. Her defence of her status within her Arab family left me realizing I knew nothing at all about the issues involved and I resolved never to raise the subject again. I suggest you do so too.

In some countries, Arab women play an increasingly important and public role in government, business and political affairs. In others, there is a long way to go before they achieve even limited recognition outside of their immediate families. That may or may not be enough to encourage you to accept that other people live the way they do because it suits them or, if it doesn't suit them, that only they can change it.

In all countries you would do well to concern yourself with what you came to do, namely to negotiate with your Arab counterpart, which means, in the main everywhere, and exclusively in some countries, that you will do business with a man. If you resent this, or can't accept it, you are unlikely to do business at all.

Hence, in Arab countries do not even think about women, let alone attempt to importune them, innocently or otherwise, and, if you must look at a camel, as I was advised in Muscat by an ex-officer of the Arab Legion, 'make sure it is a male one'!

Answers to self-assessment test 5

1   You must arrange to take as much time as is available to you if you intend to conduct business with Arabs. If your time is short (7 days) only go to one country. If you must visit them all, take at least 31 days and, if possible, another two weeks. For anything less than 28 days deduct 10 marks; for 28 days and over add 10 marks.

2   *(a)*   Never! Do not introduce a business subject with an Arab under any circumstance. Even if he is visiting you, wait for the subject to be raised by him. If he is visiting you in your own country, wait for some considerable time before raising the subject, and only then after you have exhausted

79

your 'small talk'. Never appear in a hurry to talk business and never ever appear irritated by the lack of progress in this area. (-10)

(b) Yes! (10)

3 (a) Yes. A sign of your respect for him. (10)

(b) No. It's too obvious an attempt on your part to hustle him into discussing business with you before he is ready. (-10)

(c) Absolutely not! This suggests that you are annoyed and that he is a poor host. Stick to (a) and let business take its own course. (-20)

TIPS FOR TRAVELLERS IN THE MIDDLE EAST

Check the labels on all your clothes that you are taking with you, including the ones that you are wearing for the journey. Remove any labels that come from Marks and Spencers, or any store that could be on the Arab boycott list.

Customs officers vary in the diligence with which they scan the labels to look for 'Jewish' products. It might be best if you took all labels off everything – just in case they confiscate your clothes on arrival (and note, your being in transit is no protection).

In this respect, in view of Arab sensitivity in matters connected with the state of Israel, do not attempt to travel to Arab countries with an Israeli visa stamp anywhere in your passport. You can either persuade the Israeli immigration official not to stamp your passport at all or you can apply to the authorities for two passports, one for use in visits to Israel and the other for visits to the Arab countries. The Israelis normally do not care if your passport is stamped by the Arab states.

The Middle East has more than its share of sensitive political conflicts going on at any one moment. Hence, avoid all discussions on politics, especially if you think you know something about the particular issue, and never if you know nothing about it!

Do not get into situations where you are flouting local laws, especially in matters of alcohol (watch out for expatriates who invite you to drinks parties in Saudi). The booze is doubly dangerous – it's likely to be almost pure alcohol and the police might arrive.

People who try to smuggle drugs in Turkey can spend a long time in an unpleasant jail. Likewise in Iran, where they might even execute you!

Do not deport yourself as if you have no respect for local manners, otherwise they might deport you out of the country. Immodest dress by females is highly dangerous. Disrespect to local women by males is suicidal.

Self-assessment test 6

1   You are interested in opening up business in the United States and are planning your first sales visit. You have decided to visit California first. How long do you allow yourself to meet and make presentations to potential clients:

(a)   7 days?
(b)   10 days?
(c)   21 days?
(d)   30 days?

2   You have been granted an interview with the president of a local corporation who might be interested in your product. The conversation after five minutes is still concentrated on small talk. What does this tell you?

(a)   That you are getting on fine with the other guy?
(b)   That you should raise the subject of your visit?
(c)   That you should wait for him to open the business discussion first?

3   Your (expensive and well produced) sales literature has been prepared in the UK and does you very proud in your normal negotiations. Should you:

(a)   Get it entirely re-done for your US trip?
(b)   Add in a supplement with prices quoted in US dollars?
(c)   Leave it as it is and use it as you normally do?

7 Have a good day in the US of A

or, wham, bam, it's a deal Sam

If the pace is only frantic, they're not trying

Nobody in the United States of America wants to take a long time to get a deal. They tend to make up their minds quickly. If they can't sell to you, they move off and try to sell to somebody else. They don't waste much time on the preliminaries. In fact, Americans (or more correctly, citizens of the United States – for though Uncle Sam's children are normally known as Americans, we should acknowledge that this can irritate those millions of other Americans who live south of the Rio Grande!) are probably the world's fastest dealers. They operate as if there was no tomorrow and very little left of today. They rush in (and out) where angels (and Arabs) have not even thought about fearing to tread. It's flavour of the minute rather than of the month!

This makes for a major adjustment crisis when a negotiator from Chicago meets a negotiator from almost anywhere else. The American at any one moment is likely to want to be ten moves ahead of where the negotiations have got to and, if uninitiated into the ways of those whose lives have been untouched by the Great American Reality, will probably grow impatient at the other's 'sloth'.

I have already asserted that the pace of a deal is determined by the pace of the dominant party. You cannot rush people whose instincts or bureaucratic systems require them to move crabwise or tortoise-like rather than in a full frontal assault at hare-like speed. If you want to do business with the Arabs, the Japanese, the Chinese, the South Americans, the Soviets and others, you must slow down to their pace (or speed up to it if you are even slower!).

In dealings with (US of A) Americans you most certainly must speed up, if only a little – how much depends on which of you wants the deal the most. Two Americans making a deal are a picture of haste – zap, zoom, woosh, wham, bam, let's Go Go Go! Their language colours their moves: 'Make it snappy', 'Jump to it', 'What are we waiting for?', 'Have we gotta deal, or have we gotta deal?', 'OK!, let's step on the gas!'.

The time-hustled American business executive is a model of success. Seen to be in a hurry from New York to Los Angeles is no bad thing for anybody wanting to impress his or her peers. Where the sight of the over-extended executive would worry the Japanese sick, the more over-extended he is the higher his status in downtown USA. Success is synonymous with pace. To conspicuously have too little to do is a symptom of failure, even if the American is busy doing very little.

Contrast the gentle two or three day pace of English cricket with American football. Note how North American games (ice hockey, basketball and football are prime examples) divide the match into sessions where every second, including the last, counts. If, for any reason, play stops, so does the clock; American spectators watch clocks with the same obsession that most people watch players. The entire nation is time-conscious and the ticks of passing seconds are heard right across the country. Wasting time is wasting life itself – it's unAmerican!

Think big, and then some
Haste leads to a dynamism of a special kind. The entire business world is dominated by high-energy activity. They think big and solve problems in big ways. No river is too wide for them to find a way of crossing it. Where most people would make do with a single bridge, they think nothing of having a dozen. They let competition sort out the appropriate level of a service. Their economy is on a grand scale – the world's largest at several trillion dollars a year.

They use up and spew out resources at a rate that is truly astonishing. They have created vast cities with urban and suburban sprawls that dwarf, on all indicators (good and bad), those of the rest of the world. Their prairies are larger than entire countries and their natural resources are the envy of the world. They feed themselves and much of the world too. By their economic strength they can afford to buy up the greater proportion of the natural resources that they don't have from those parts of the world that do. In short, the US of A is an El Dorado. It knows it, and much of the world resents it; yet all the world wants to emulate it!

Go into any up country village and you will find ordinary people who describe their desires in terms common to the (somewhat dated and often phoney) image of the USA that they get from TV or the movies. Whereas political leaders may aspire to economic development, measured in terms of steel tonnage or national airlines, the ordinary people think in terms of coca-cola, consumer goods and large cars.

The very size of the US market means that their international negotiators usually are interested only in the very largest of contracts (Bechtel's contracts, for instance, are very big). For this reason, US international negotiators tend to deal with national governments – for whom, incidentally, the annual value of the output of the companies they negotiate with is quite awesome when set against their own country's GNP.

This is not to say that the US negotiators get it all their own way. Many is the tale told by experienced US negotiators that lists the irritations they have suffered at the obfuscation, delay, bureaucratic ineptitude, sheer bloody-mindedness and, in their view, ultimately self-defeating obstruction of a national government agency, when thay have tried to put together a mega (or super-mega) deal. Their frustration is enhanced when they consider the project to be of mutual benefit to the US company and the (often) poorer country. Whereas profits motivate a US company, the politics of resentment and suspicion (naturally) dominate a government's negotiating policy. These differing objectives can conflict in ways that inhibit successful negotiation – and the world as a whole is poorer for it.

Quick deals

Doing quick deals has several drawbacks. The most obvious is that it is easier to make mistakes, especially ones that in due course you will regret. This adds another dimension to negotiating with US companies: they are more than a trifle litigious. At the drop of a subpoena they will have you in court, and never for trivial damages!

You miss a delivery which costs a client $10,000 and he will sue you for $10 million. Fail to shape up to a partnership or agency agreement and you will be chased for half of your country's GNP. This makes the US of A a haven for smart lawyers (not to mention doctors, psychiatrists and marketing specialists). Fortunately, lawyers are not prejudiced – they will sue other lawyers, even for malpractice.

85

But the business atmosphere is one of constant upheaval. They do quick deals quicker than anybody else, then they engage in further deals to get out from under the deals they have done. Promises are extravagant before the sale (marketing and advertising are true US art forms) and negotiators work hard (and fast) to get the deal set up. In other places that would be the end of the matter but in the US of A a whole world of after-sales negotiating exists because of the risks arising from the before-the-sale deal. Only in the US of A is the threat that a politician could be a used car salesman a serious warning that you ought not to vote for him!

Indeed, look at any American text on negotiating (they call it 'self-improvement') and you will see much attention paid to negotiating your grievances with the people with whom you have recently done business. It's not just 'how to get a discount' but 'how to get it fixed when it (inevitably) breaks down'.

Handling grievances, complaining, getting refunds, suing the suppliers and generally fighting for your corner are all par for the course in American negotiating. The expectation is that sooner or later deals will go wrong in some way, because making deals faster means making more deals.

Instead of slowing down the process of getting into a deal they recommend that the parties indulge in 'self-assertion' therapy. To assert oneself in a noisy marketplace means, when all else is stripped away, becoming noisier oneself. Instead of meekly accepting the deal that you made, you are encouraged to assert your rights in no uncertain way.

Most US citizens interpret firmness and certainty as being synonymous with shouting and talking quickly. Hence, they repeat the behaviour – only more exaggerated – that got them into the lousy deal in the first place: they talk and shout quickly. Of course, the other guy shouts back and we have a typical North American version of a Mediterranean street row.

The US school of negotiating

Now there is no point complaining about the quick kill school of negotiating. The US of A is not going to change its behaviour merely because you think it ought to do so. The American way is, for better or worse, the way it is and you must adjust to it. The American negotiator is not as subtle as, say, the Japanese. Being in a hurry, the American has to try to bring things to a head in the

LOVE ME, LOAD MY DOG

I saw a guy at O'Hare airport, Chicago, shouting like a barrack room sergeant at a new recruit, and complaining vividly, complete with gesticulations of a kind that would have made Mussolini envious, at the damage done to a dog crate by somebody loading or unloading the plane. The dog was slunked into one corner (presumably having heard his master in full throttle more than once) and, to put it mildly, the crate stank (suggesting, perhaps, that it had been dropped when the loaders carrying it had fainted!).

The airport official, a quiet lady in uniform, stood there listening to the tirade but otherwise appeared unperturbed by it, and kept calling calmly on her personal radio for the supervisor.

When the supervisor arrived, she told the loaders to move the crate from the area, at which the irate guy blew his top even more. Nothing, apparently, was to be moved until his lawyer got there and the airline boss arrived and paid compensation ('the damn dog cost me six thousand bucks and the crate is evidence that you've tried to kill it').

Having not much to do, I (and about a hundred others) watched the scene with interest. The guy had a point but his manner seemed a trifle absurd to me – even counterproductive – and I thought he should be concentrating on his proposed remedy (compensation) rather than competing for an Oscar for dramatic acting.

You will not, however, negotiate in the US of A for long before you come across a version of the dog owner at O'Hare. You will also learn not to take the dog owner type too seriously, or too personally. To the uninitiated, the dog owner's behaviour is pure intimidation. It is the verbal equivalent of the massive damages claim put in by his lawyers to scare the timid into a quick settlement. Courts do it too. They set you up for ninety-nine years in jail and then let you plea-bargain it down to six months suspended!

shortest possible time and he (or, of course, she) will do this by a combination of apparent confidence, to persuade you of their integrity (hence the significance of their question: 'Would you buy a used car from this man?'), and early use of whatever power, or, as they call it, leverage, that they have in the relationship to compel you to accept what they are proposing.

They love to impress upon you just how powerful they are. They can do this by emphasizing the sheer size of their company – 'the biggest in Texas' – in terms of market share, billion dollar sales, or numbers of employees. When you are in the presence of a US executive from a multi-billion dollar company you are not likely to be left unaware that doing business with him is in your best interest.

The United States contains many of the world's largest corporations. Indeed, to be large is regarded as being very American, and they identify their corporate interests very closely with the interests of their country: 'What's good for America is good for General Motors'.

Large corporations do not lose their competitive edge in the US environment (though it has to be said that the largest US firms are a long way from being competitive in the literal sense). The giant corporations play a very hard game, with little quarter shown or expected between rivals. The government has curtailed some of the worst excesses of the abuse of corporate power by regulation and recently has resorted to exposing US corporations to more competition.

Being large they have room for some market failures and can ride out a disaster or two. Big deals are set up by teams of managers who work extremely hard and very thoroughly to develop a negotiating position. They will decide on a policy that suits their own best interests and then push hard for it.

If you are selling, they will go strong on the size of the market in the United States and, therefore, why you should do business with them, emphasizing gross sales and revenues. If you are buying, they will go strong on the sheer size of their world-wide sales and, therefore, why you should do business with them, emphasizing their total service and how much profit you can make.

This approach will also hint at whether you think you are big enough (macho?) to do business on a scale and at a high enough standard that their operation requires. You can even get the feeling that they are doing you a favour!

Prepared contracts

The US negotiator operates in a world of prepared contracts or 'established' systems of doing business. Because they have one eye on what happens if the deal goes sour, they protect themselves with legal ploys. They also tend to have a monopolistic attitude to doing business: they believe, and get you to believe, that you need them more than they need you. To some extent this is true, because with a three trillion dollar economy to play with there is always somebody else available who could do the job you want to do, if the price is right.

Car hire firms insist that you sign their pre-printed hire forms; repair and maintenance services make you sign standard contracts; you sign forms to get on a plane (less now since the shuttle and de-regulation), to book a room in a hotel, or to place an order for anything.

A whole mountain of pre-printed forms exists that require your signature to get a lot of things done. It's a protective device to ensure that you have signed away your rights (or, at least had them severely curtailed). For this reason you must read the paperwork very carefully – and take your time about it too! If you disagree with anything, tell them and refuse to sign until it is changed. The impression that you cannot change a printed form is a form of intimidation (that's why it is pre-printed).

They will tell you that this or that 'rule' applies to delivery, minimum orders, payments and so on. If you find these 'rules' onerous, challenge them. If there is one country in the world where they make a meal out of legal issues it is the United States (they have a large – and prosperous – legal system of which they are proud and they think it is very patriotic to use it).

They have an aversion to 'one truck contracts' and prefer to ask themselves beforehand hundreds of 'what if?' type questions. According to their answers, they develop fairly tight working contracts and attempt to foist these on to you at every negotiation. Such contracts can protect you too, but you can never be sure that the other guy had your interests uppermost in his mind while preparing his standard contract.

The role of testimonials

Operating under the permanent threat of litigation (or, as it seems sometimes, the threat of permanent litigation!) and also at great speed, the US negotiator has developed a special form of semi-

NEVER MIND THE WIDTH, FEEL THE QUALITY

The US of A triumphs in one area above all others: technological excellence. They are world leaders in the application of technology and have enough economic strength to buy in what they do not discover themselves. With the world's richest market available to exploit any innovation, they can afford to try out almost anything, and often do (California, for instance, institutionalizes new 'crazes' – it is also the home of the original silicon valley).

Hence, the US of A buys in a lot of semi-manufactured components. Its computer manufacturers, for instance, buy in circuit boards from places as disparate as Taiwan, Scotland, Singapore, Germany and Yugoslavia (open up the back of yours and check where the bits on the boards come from – it's a veritable lesson in geography).

To negotiate a trade deal with a large US company you must have two things going for you: first, you have to have a sensible price policy, for if you don't they will manufacture your parts themselves with their very expensive but highly productive labour; second, you must reach and maintain a high consistency in quality and you had better believe they want high quality in actual performance and not just in your promises.

Now if you satisfy these two conditions you can negotiate a profitable deal with a US company. But that is just the beginning of their requirements of you. They will always be looking for volume – the US of A is no place for a backyard business – for they operate on a scale almost inconceivable abroad (with the possible exception of the more enlightened of the multinational companies – often US – operating in the EEC).

Next, but by no means least, they will expect you to seek to reduce unit costs, to improve the product, to be in the forefront, without prompting, of making suggestions for alternative ways of doing whatever it is that you do best. Hence you do not just sell to the US customer, you must learn to market your product as well.

insurance, that is, the full blown testimonial. They do this more than anybody else and it is a feature of the US business scene.

From the day they graduate from High School (and then again from College or University), the US business executive has a place somewhere on the wall for the Diploma, complete with a class picture. This identifies the executive as a regular guy.

If service in the armed forces was required then some sign of that achievement will also feature somewhere in the room (preferably a signed picture by a famous General or Admiral). Again, if the executive served under or has known a top politician – the Governor of the state, the Congressman or even the Senator – a picture of the two of them together is a kosher testimonial. (Naturally, acquaintance with a President is the highest acolade, worth at least three photos of the executive with a Vice-President!)

The wall displays are there to establish the executive in the subtle hierarchy of established US society. There are also the more mobile testimonials in the form of letters of commendation for the executive or for the products of his corporation from the top executives of client companies. No presentation to a US company from somebody who wants to do business with them is complete without a sheaf of testimonials written by other major users of the product.

This, of course, can create a problem for a new company trying to break into the US market. Most of us have known the Catch-22 situation of trying to sell a new product for a new company, when the client says: 'Who have you sold this to before?' and you have to admit that he is (nearly) the first customer. It sure weakens your negotiating position when you cannot show that everybody but everybody has bought your product before. Unless you get clients you cannot establish a track record for your product, but you cannot get clients unless you have a track record.

You will also find it worthwhile to carry with you in the USA a master copy of your *cv* for clients to photocopy. They like to know with whom they are dealing.

The overseas negotiator about to visit the US on a selling trip would be well advised to prepare a bundle of testimonials from the highest levels of the clients that are already on his books in Europe. And do not weary of collecting them after the first half dozen – there is no limit to the appetite of US customers for reading testimonials from 'names' that they recognize.

The reason is quite simple: the testimonial of a company president that your product is first class and that doing business with you is good for his business is evidence (though not conclusive) that a deal with you is not going to end in ruinous litigation. The absence of testimonials is evidence that you are a large risk.

The market

The entire US economy is dominated by a freer market than is found anywhere else in the world. True, the US government, and the state governments, account for immense expenditures of billions of dollars, and these expenditures are major inputs into the economy. But the driving force behind the US economy is the competitive urge that motivates millions of people to take risks and seek their fortunes.

Whereas the average communist state official is notoriously risk averse (for, it should be said, the best possible of motivations – self-preservation!), the average US commercial buyer or seller is inclined to accept risk in return for the prospect of material reward. And the rewards are substantial. Already experiencing high living standards, represented by astonishing buying power, the US citizen functions in an atmosphere of self-improvement by effort and opportunity to reach even higher living standards.

If one thing does not work, they will try something else. Americans are highly mobile with regard to business propositions. Below the huge corporations, which are huge because they do something that works, there are literally millions of guys (of both sexes!) seeking to break through to the big money. This makes the US market the most exciting, and the most ruthless, in the world.

An entire range of behaviour exists purporting to guide the US citizen who is on the make. Much of this sounds quite vulgar and not a little crude to European ears. The litany includes the kind of tough talking advice that Hollywood scriptwriters (themselves on highly tenuous work contracts that probably influence their view of American values) have made famous in their one-liners in a thousand movies: 'Nice guys come second'; 'When the going gets tough, the tough get going'; 'Shape up or ship out'; 'You get what you pay for'; 'There ain't no such thing as a free lunch'; 'If you have to ask how much it costs, you can't afford it!'; 'If you're so smart, why ain't you rich?' and so on.

ATTENTION TO DETAIL

The US economy is competitive. This has produced an entirely professional approach to how US companies view proposals from overseas negotiators. If what you are offering is available from any of a hundred other companies you will have a hard time convincing them to do business with you.

A British real estate partnership, which had developed some business with clients moving to and from New York, decided to tackle the US market direct.

The US real estate business is saturated with sizeable operations of high professional standards, and it is also flooded with low quality brokers who give real estate broking a sour name.

Clearly, to break into the lucrative market the UK company had to establish its professional credentials and rise above the pack. It did this by an example of professionalism that matched the best available in the New York market.

For five months, day in day out, the new team trudged the streets of Manhattan, up and down *every* office building in the city, making a register of all office lets. True they could have bought this information from an agency but they wanted their people to have an unrivalled knowledge of the city's buildings and the facilities. They also accumulated a mass of information from janitors, security staff and employees on who was moving soon, which floors were empty and what the neighbourhoods were really like.

Every bit of useful information was put onto a computer. Scores of hours were spent digesting potential moves and vacancies. As the information built up, the search for clients commenced. People who had complained of being too crowded, etc., where they were, had information supplied at no charge on where something more suitable was located.

Slowly the business built up until they were established as leading negotiators for anybody who had an interest in New York property. Within two years they were the most successful overseas partnership in the company, firmly established in the toughest, and richest, market in the world. They got big by being better.

Winners and losers

Even in their approach to negotiating Americans are obsessed with 'winning'. A well-known seminar series in the US is entitled 'Winning the Negotiation', and even my own work has not been immune to this treatment. When a US firm published *Managing Negotiations* (1981) (written with my co-authors, John Benson and John McMillan) they subtitled it: 'a guide for managers, labor leaders, politicians and *everyone else who wants to win*'.

The US of A is the land of winners and losers. For the winners there is nothing too good for them; for the losers there is nothing. And there is certainly nothing like the sweet smell of success, and for a sniff of this sweet smell, US citizen give it their 'best shot'.

Now it would be grievously unfair to leave the impression that the US of A was peopled by several million psychopaths who cared little for each other and even less for you. Nothing could be further from the truth. The US manner, outlined above, is by no means as serious as it sounds when you first come across it. The US citizen is often misunderstood – by and large they are a very warm and generous people who establish enduring relationships in business and life that will match anything this side of Shangri-la.

The tough language, the winner-takes-all outlook, the 'get off your ass and get going' philosophy, these are modes of expression for their competitive urge in their lives. They are by no means a final statement of their morality or ethics.

If you bring professionalism to your presentation, sheer excellence in your quality control and realistic prices that suit their market philosophy (high initial prices with room for discounts and frequent 'special offers', sales and such-like), and can deliver what you promise in quantities that will make you gasp, then you will get the business you deserve.

The first forty-five seconds

The US negotiator expects to get to the point quickly. A real estate broker I know in New York tells his guys that when they get an interview with a potential client they have forty-five seconds to make a hit or blow it. In comparison, the approach of the Arab or Japanese negotiator is distinctly soporific. But the rewards of getting it right in the US of A are truly tremendous. So watch your first forty-five seconds – you may not have the guy's attention for the rest of your first and only minute!

BIG IS BEAUTIFUL

The US economy – the largest in the world – is worth over three trillion dollars a year, of which about 10 per cent is made up of imports (compared to over 30 per cent in the UK). This is both an opportunity – for ten per cent of three trillion is an awful lot of business – and a problem – for with 90 per cent of output produced within the US, you have a lot of local competition. The market is so big that it is unlikely that you can cover it all from scratch.

The nearest area to Europe is around the North East (New York and Boston), and the industrial complex running from Philadelphia through New York is the world's largest.

The furthest area from Europe is also the largest and fastest growing market. California has a population of 24 million, mainly affluent, people, whose average income exceeds the US national average. Los Angeles alone is so large that it would cover the area between Brighton and Cambridge and Slough to Southend.

Another 28 million Americans live in the sunbelt South-West (Texas etc.) and their economy thrives from oil, agribusiness, defence, technology and leisure. Other huge markets exist in the Mid-West (Chicago to St Louis, Minneapolis/St Paul to Pittsburg – an area about six times larger than the UK), the South-East (the two Carolinas to Florida), the North-West (Washington to Wyoming) and the Mid-Atlantic (contiguous with Washington DC).

To succeed in these markets you must be well prepared. The US attitude to sales promotion is altogether different – they spend more time and money promoting their products than is normal elsewhere. If you want them to distribute your products they will expect to get financial help (how much?) with the (high) costs of promotion; they will expect substantial stocks to be available within the US (where and at what share of the risk?); and they will try for 'sole and exclusive rights' (for how long and on what terms?). And you must price everything in US dollars (so open with high prices and don't be intimidated because it sounds a lot!). By the time they have stripped your prices for discounts you will be glad you took my advice.

TIPS FOR TRAVELLERS IN THE USA

The basic rule of business is: you get what you pay for. If you go cheaply you can expect to suffer inconvenience. Only the very wealthy avoid the hassles and the crowds. Hence, select on service as well as price.

Avoid Kennedy Airport as a gateway into the USA. The immigration authorities are notoriously slow. Everybody queues for ages – an hour is no exception – to be interviewed by a generally friendly, but never speedy, immigration official. At Kennedy the service is worse than almost anywhere else. You will have to change terminals to change planes, and the chaos of the baggage halls, the inter-terminal bus service, and the general mayhem make the disembarkation onto the beaches at Dunkirk a monument to order and decorum.

Since deregulation of air-traffic, there are planes taking off from everywhere to everywhere else, usually at the same time. This means there can be delays – two or more hours – during peak travel, so allow for it in your plans. The view from the plane of the local runway is boring after an hour, so get an aisle seat.

Do not go for walks in downtown areas late at night. Take a taxi no matter how short the distance. Even early morning joggers have been mugged (by other joggers!), and late night strollers will have their wealth, if not their features, redistributed for them.

The standard of service, even in the most modest of establishments, is generally much higher than in Europe. While US citizens can be extremely noisy, they are, in the main, very polite. People serving you with almost anything will do so as if they enjoy it and want to please you.

US citizens, even recent ones, are patriotic. They do not like to be called 'Colonials', or have their institutions mocked. They are not collectively responsible for their TV programmes, Hollywood versions of World War II, US tourists abroad, and organized crime. Hence, avoid provocation!

Answers to self-assessment test 6

1 (a) Far too short given the huge distances that you will have to fly/drive around California (there is no public transport worth mentioning). It's not the time they take to negotiate (usually much shorter than anybody else) but the sheer size of the USA that determines the time you should make available. (-10)

   (b) Still too short to see enough people to justify your trip. You are bound to want/need to return and a ten-day trip will only tease the market. (-5)

   (c) Much better. You can see several clients in twenty-one days spread across the state or even across Los Angeles. (3)

   (d) Ideal (and possibly longer if you can). The more time you can spend examining this market the better. It is huge and there are so many people trying to get on to the road to riches that you need time to check them out, and to count your fingers every time you shake hands with a guy who is going 'to make your dreams come true'. (10)

2 (a) If you are still stuck in small talk anything beyond a minute, either he is a long lost relative or you and your deal are dead. He is bound to be wondering how he is going to get you out of his office and his sight. (-10)

   (b) Absolutely. You had better get on with it. The fact that you are still there talking to him about nothing in particular suggests that the buzzer under his desk that he has been pressing for his security gorillas to come and chuck you out is not working. Tell him what you want, NOW! (10)

   (c) If you wait much longer he will throw you out himself, so you had better not wait for him to raise the subject of business. Go for (b) NOW. (-15)

3 (a) Absolutely correct. Even if it costs you everything you have already paid for the UK version, get a new set done for the US market, preferably through an agency that knows the US market. Their standards are higher. (10)

   (b) A poor alternative to (a) but much better than (c). US citizens are totally incapable of understanding anybody else's currency but their own and on their own ground they will not even attempt to do so. If you quote in sterling pounds you might as well stay at home and save the airfare. (3)

   (c) You are about to waste your airfare. (-10)

Self-assessment test 7

1 You are engaged in social conversation with your business partners in Bogata. The discussion drifts to the subject of Latin American economic development. Do you:

(a) Avail yourself of the opportunity to discourse on the comparative social and political differences between North and South America in the 19th century?

(b) Ask your partners for their views but offer none yourself?

(c) Ask them why California and other former regions of Mexico have done so well as part of the United States compared to their mother country?

(d) Suggest that South America needs social and political reforms to generate a successful capitalism?

2 You are in Rio de Janeiro making preliminary enquiries to select a local agent for your laser machines. You speak poor Spanish. Do you:

(a) Have a go at speaking Spanish to your contacts?

(b) Refrain from doing so and concentrate solely on English?

3 You are looking for ways to sell your products in Venezuela and you are approached by a merchant in Caracas who offers to represent you in the entire country. Do you:

(a) Sign a contract with him after checking out his financial standing?

(b) Ask him whom else he represents?

8 Similarity in diversity
or, doing deals south of the Rio Grande

Slow down

If citizens of the United States seldom take a long time to do a deal, citizens of the Americas south of the Rio Grande seldom do a deal, or much else, quickly, and if there is one thing that they dislike, it is being pushed about by Europeans or rushed around by 'wham, bam, it's a deal, Sam' negotiators from the North.

While you are rushing in, South Americans are still trying to get to know you. When you are thinking in billions, they are thinking in millions, and perhaps hundreds of thousands. When you want to sign up the entire continent for your wonderful products, they concern themselves with the minute portion they can handle within their national territory. Some multinationals have total world sales greater than the GNP of some South American countries.

You are going to have to slow down the pace of your negotiations, or attempts at negotiation, with business managers in Central and South America, and probably scale down your volume numbers too.

It's always difficult coming from a large economy to a smaller one. There is a natural irritation (seldom disguised by being patronizing) at a person who thinks smaller than you do, but remember the guy thinks smaller because he and his business opportunities are smaller. It's probably more difficult for a deal to be struck between a negotiator in Bolivia and a negotiator in Chile than it is for you to visit both places and do two separate deals.

If you learn to slow down the pace of your business life, you will probably end up doing more business than you will if you don't.

Save your high energy output for the tiring flight between Mexico City and Ezeiza airport, Buenos Aires, and save your breath for your business trip to La Paz in Bolivia, where you'll need it just for the journey from the taxi to the foyer of the Plaza hotel (you're

12,500 feet above sea level and you'll feel as if you have jogged all the way from Al Alto airport carrying your bag – two bags will kill you!).

Don't look down
Above all else, learn to avoid giving the impression that you are doing them any favours by offering them deals in the first place.

Citizens south of the Rio Grande have an ambivalent attitude to Europe and the United States: they admire, indeed, covet, their material wealth but don't have much time for what they regard as the insensitivity, almost arrogance, of some of their citizens with whom they come into contact. This insensitivity is not confined to US citizens. Many Europeans are just as bad, if not even more appalling, in their business manners and more than one deal has died as a result.

Negative perceptions about the USA and Europe are often unfair but they are nevertheless widespread. Latin Americans are very proud of their national identities. Their countries may well be poorer than yours, their political systems may often be less than democratic, their comparative performance with the USA in the years since the 18th century may not cast them in the best light, and their people may be sharply divided into haves and have-nots on a scale seldom seen elsewhere, but they are as emotionally attached to their countries, manifest failings and all, and with a passion no less deeply felt, as the most red-blooded of Europeans to their history.

Some negotiators visiting Central and South America for the first time require considerable effort to set aside their innocent unintended biases and their pre-determined stereotypes, and treat the people with whom they hope to do business with the respect and equality that they deserve (and seek). Almost without being conscious of it, the 'first-timer' (and not a few of the 'old hands') can slip into attitudes and verbal asides that rub the Latin American the wrong way, much to the detriment of the business that they might have done if a more sensitive posture had been even half as obvious as their rude one.

Don't look back
South Americans do not take kindly to lectures by Europeans on how they might have done it all better if only they had done it the same way as the pioneers of the North. They are well aware that the

social and political institutions of South America have not always helped their development processes but they are just as aware that these social and political institutions are part of their countries' heritages, for good or evil, and are as valuable to their societies as social stabilizers as are those institutions revered by people in the United States. Some of their capital cities were founded before the Pilgrim Fathers had the first Thanksgiving dinner with the local Indians.

They certainly do not regard their pasts with unmitigated shame and resent having an often ignorant version of their history shoved down their throats — even politely — by people who share as many guilts about the North American Indian, the Australian Aborigine, and the black slave trade, as they are alleged to do about the Indians. It is salutary to note that many of the peoples of these countries are pure-blood Indians or mixed Indian-Spanish (e.g. Bolivia, Colombia, Peru, Paraguay, Venezuela) and these proud peoples have demonstrated an ethnic integration and survival rate that contrasts remarkably well with that of the indigenous peoples of North America, or Australia, or, for that matter, the non-Russian peoples of Siberia.

Every mix of ethnic composition is found in South America. The proportion of European stock runs from the almost totally European populations of Argentina and Uruguay, through Brazil's 60 per cent to Chile's 30 per cent, Venezuela's 20 per cent, and Peru's 11 per cent. The balance varies between pure-blooded Amerindian, Mestizos (mixed Spanish-Indian), Creoles (part African descent), Asian Indians and Mulattoes.

If you are doing business in South America you could be negotiating with someone from almost any racial group, but if you remember that you are the outsider, the 'foreigner', the 'gringo' (and some Latins can say 'gringo' in a way that makes clear they have been insulted in the past by another gringo!), you will have no difficulty on racial grounds.

The men, or less likely the women, with whom you are negotiating, whatever their racial origins or mixtures, are at home in their societies, and, because they will be rich by definition — only the rich negotiate with the business gringos, for only the rich have the wherewithal to do a deal — they will be respected in their societies for being rich, if for nothing else. It is not skin colour that counts in Latin America, it is wealth and position.

WITH FRIENDS LIKE THESE . . .

An Argentinian business leader was visiting Washington DC to meet with various senators who were in favour of strong US-Argentinian relations. He met with the staff of one senator who had long been prominent in promoting good relations between US and Argentinian business leaders.

It was not long before the subject of the Argentinian economy came up and the high rate of inflation that was afflicting it. The Argentinian explained the political and economic background to his country's inflation problems and dealt with the legacy of the Peron years and how the military governments had not been very competent in dealing with the real issues.

A member of the senator's staff told the visitor that 'if we could run your country for eighteen months, we would soon turn it round'. He took the silence that followed as an invitation to continue with his thoughts on how the USA would run Argentina better than the Argentinians.

He did not know it then (though the senator made it abundantly clear later), but making such statements was likely to do more damage to US-Argentinian relations in ten minutes than some critics of Argentina could manage in a lifetime. And no amount of reference by the senator's aide to the Falklands as the Malvinas compensated for the derogatory implications of his remarks.

Argentinians, in common with most people everywhere else, do not take kindly to foreigners who insult them. Of course, people who understand their own country's problems, and are honest enough to talk about them with foreigners, risk, though they do not invite, ignorant 'know-alls' telling them how much better they could run their economies in 'eighteen months'.

But for a so-called friend of Argentina to make this mistake shows just how easy it is to sink a negotiation by thoughtless remarks.

Mind your own business

On the economic front, a country like Brazil, where whatever else occasionally torments its people racism does not, if it follows present trends will become one of the world's top five economies as measured by GNP. Mexico, Argentina, and Venezuela, whatever the problems of the past, are by no means inevitably excluded from a sound economic future, and they have much to be proud of (and know it) in what they have achieved already. In sum, the 21st century may well be the time when Latin America comes into its own.

At present you are negotiating with people who live in a continent diverse in circumstance, environment and outlook, yet similar in history, opportunity and way of life.

The legacy of the Spanish and Portuguese, who colonized the greater part of the continent, is everywhere to be seen in the languages they speak (Portuguese in Brazil, Spanish everywhere else, albeit with a local hemispheric intonation), and in the institution of the Roman Catholic Church (with tolerated 'add-ons' from indigenous Indian and slave trade peoples' religions).

Similar legacies of the past on a much smaller scale can be seen in the French, Dutch and British former colonies of Central and South America and the Caribbean islands.

The South American political structure is a Latin and, thereby, manqué version of the American Revolution against European colonialism. The early 19th-century independence revolutions against Spain and Portugal did not lead to a 'United States of South America' − despite the hopes of such as Simon Bolivar − but led instead to a score of separate national states, each duplicating the apparatus of statehood (armed forces, customs barriers, state currencies, legal systems, etc.) and forgoing the benefits of a large market (free trade in goods and free movement of peoples).

With this background in mind, keep your views on the world to yourself and, above all else, mind your own business about how they run their country. You are out to trade your goods for cash, or vice versa, not to embark on a career as a nation reformer. The first task is difficult enough, the latter futile. You might as well try to sell booze and pork cutlets to the Arabs as interfere gratuitously in the politics of a South American country. You are there to negotiate for your business, not to take sides.

Anyway, there are radicals aplenty trying to change South America from the inside (they live there!), and nobody needs advice from you on how to run things 'better'. If you're interested in politics, stand for election in your own country; don't try to combine this with a business career in South America.

Moreover, and this is pure Latin American, many members of the richer layers of their societies, with whom you might be negotiating, favour various degrees of change in the way their countries run their affairs too, and you can never be sure that the guy you are mouthing off at is not sympathetic to the very changes taking place in his country that you are denouncing.

You are there to do business, so keep to that agenda. Otherwise you may end up being told whose business to mind and how far away in the world you should mind it.

Less than free trade

One great and immediately obvious contrast between doing business in South America and doing business in the United States is the consequence of a continent consisting of 13 separate countries (21 if Central America and 34 if the Caribbean are included) instead of just two. Europeans should feel at home in these circumstances!

A Texan wanting to export her products to other parts of the United States need do no more than comply with the same federal laws that govern her in Texas (with minor differences in state zoning and taxation perhaps). She will also get paid in the currency that she pays her own employees — the US dollar.

The same Texan wanting to export her products south of the Rio Grande will confront 21 different commercial laws and regulations, 21 different taxation systems and 21 different customs procedures.

If she manages to get paid in US dollars she will still have to convert her prices into local currencies, some of which sound the same but aren't (for example, pesos in Bolivia, Chile, Colombia, Uruguay and Argentina) and some of which don't and still aren't (e.g. the bolivar in Venuezuela, guarani in Paraguay, sol in Peru, sucre in Ecuador, and cruzeiro in Brazil). There are also some which sound familiar (the franc in French Guiana, dollar in Guyana and gilder in Surinam).

Foreign currencies are a bewildering topic even to bankers. If different rates of inflation are taken into account, the exchange rates between them and your currency are an additional complication, and this can have some significance when negotiating a deal.

A consignment of electrical switch-gear has a different value to an exporter if the deal is cost, insurance and freight (CIF) to a warehouse in Buenaventura in Colombia instead of free on board (FOB), Tilbury, UK.

This problem is compounded if the CIF price is quoted to a place like Rosario in Argentina where inflation has recently been hitting 400 per cent a year and inflation-ridden port labour charges alone could eliminate the profit unless compensated by severe and frequent devaluations of the peso.

This gives international negotiators something else to think about on top of the many other things they must consider. It's not just the price that is important, it's where and when it becomes due and at what exchange rate and who pays for associated services in other currencies.

From a negotiator's point of view, the deal should be denominated in your own currency, leaving inflationary and exchange rate fluctuations as a problem exclusively for the other guy, and should be FOB, leaving shipping costs and risks to the importer.

Customs regulations in some countries (such as Brazil) will assess tariff rates on the CIF value of the goods irrespective of what terms they are traded upon. If they catch you, or suspect you of, 'mistakenly' under-valuing your goods you could be penalized by a doubling of the tariff duty. In some countries you must enter the CIF and the FOB prices on the invoice irrespective of who is paying the difference.

But whatever happens a negotiator must keep the deal in his own currency — if anything goes wrong he can still pay his own costs. Bags full of a foreign currency may sound OK at today's exchange rate but be nothing but bags full of paper in a year's time.

Naturally, the business community of South America have alerted their governments to the vagaries of international trade and these governments have passed laws that aim to assist their own negotiators — though their net effect is to restrain trade.

Generally, imports are regarded by the protectionist-minded as less attractive than exports. (Free trade is less than free and nowhere is this more true than in South America.) Commercial regulations based on this prejudice always end up — whatever the intentions of the legislators — inhibiting trade. Such proposals are *always* presented as being in the 'national' interest but always and everywhere they are in the interests of a minority of business people.

Paperwork as an import barrier

Whole batteries of import licence regulations exist in several countries, and they will be fired off at you no matter how big a favour you think you are doing to a country by selling it advanced technology and products that will do it nothing but good.

You can get your goods to the port in, say, Colombia and still not get them through customs until stringent formalities are completed. In truth you have little to complain about because EEC customs are formality-ridden too.

Typically, and not the least of it, your opposite number will have to pay into his country's central bank between 40 and 60 per cent of the peso value of the goods you are selling to him. That is just to get the goods out of customs and into his hands.

From his side of the negotiating table this legal requirement for a prior deposit acts to inhibit him from importing goods that he is not fairly sure of selling. This thus inhibits the taking of risks and the entrepreneurial seizure of opportunities. As he can never be sure of selling anything in advance, he must put pressure on your prices and has every incentive to do so, apart from it being a basic negotiating stance common the world over.

The import deposit law precludes him from making advance payments to you. He would be crazy to agree to payments on account unless you accepted payment in his local currency, which would suggest you were crazy too, or certainly desperate. His country's laws push him into a tough bargaining stance whether he is temperamentally geared up to do so or not – and South Americans can be just as astute as you when it comes to the terms of your mutual deal.

Meanwhile, your goods are sitting in a South American warehouse and you have not yet been paid a penny. The risk for title to your goods is carried by you, and there is not a lot you can do about it. If you decide not to take such a risk – and you are always free so to do – you will trade elsewhere, which is what is intended by those who promoted these trading laws (and variations on them found across the world).

You won't get closer to getting paid unless and until your trading partner deposits at his state bank various certificates, including the import licence he should have obtained before ordering the goods (did he do this?), your invoice (which must have absolutely *no* mistakes on it, even typographical ones, so make sure your translation is perfect), and a letter from him, countersigned by his

HEAR THIS, IMPORTERS!

Many Latin American countries actively discourage imports. Just to make sure that you and your potential partners get the message, the country's government will give you the prospect of paying all kinds of taxes just for the privilege of selling goods to people who want to buy them but not at any price.

Brazil is a classic example of the application of disincentives to import (Mexico was for long another example). Assuming your products are not on the long list of *national similars* (things that can be produced in Brazil), they would be liable to the following duties before you can sell them to the otherwise happy Brazilians:

1 A tariff *ad valorem* on the CIF value decided by a government customs *official* (i.e. not by you or your Brazilian partner).

2 A tax on the foreign exchange transaction required by your Brazilian partner if he is to pay you in your own currency.

3 A federal manufactured goods tax calculated on the 'duty paid', not CIF, value.

4 A state merchandise circulation tax calculated on the duty *plus* all other taxes paid value.

5 A 3 per cent *ad valorem* port charge (which includes the 'Port Improvement Tax').

6 A 2 per cent *ad valorem* CIF warehousing charge plus all customs inspection and paperwork expenses.

7 A 20 per cent of the cost of freight charge to the Merchant Marine Fund.

8 A 2 percent *ad valorem* CIF customs broker's commission.

9 Finally a levy of 10 per cent on the customs broker's commission to be paid to the broker's union.

bank, that he owes you the money for the goods you have sent to him.

But you still don't get your money! About three weeks later, the importer applies to the exchange registration office (or equivalent in his country) for a licence to pay you in foreign currency. Several weeks later — or even longer! — he should receive permission to purchase foreign exchange for remittance to you.

He will now have to pay his bank its commission for handling the transaction and the balance owing on the goods above the deposit he made, perhaps, several months earlier when they arrived at his country's port; that is, when you completed your end of the deal.

As a negotiator you are boxed in to some extent. Not only can you not get him to agree to pay you in advance, even a small deposit, but you cannot hold on to title to your goods once he applies to clear them through customs. How fast he sells them in his country is not in your hands, but his, and naturally if sales are sluggish he has an incentive not to process the import and exchange formalities as fast as you might be anxious for him to do.

You can opt for a letter of credit type of transaction, but this will cost you bank charges for arranging it. It will also be fixed at a minimum of 90 days. The question as to which way you are paid fastest is something which only hindsight will tell you!

Try padding your prices

I would not go so far as to suggest that every deal you make is subject to 'administrative' delays which cover up his (temporary) commercial embarrassments, but you certainly are vulnerable to these delays. Therefore you must seek to negotiate deals only with the soundest of business partners. This usually means large rather than small South American businesses and products that have a fairly certain demand, such as high-value machinery for a government contract, and preferably one that has some 'political protection' and diplomatic leverage close to it.

The worst thing for you to do when faced with these delays is to agree to re-negotiate the price of the deal, just to get some of your money. There is a temptation to do so — not that they need suggest this to you. You would not be worth much as a negotiator if you did not automatically think of this option when reading the above paragraphs.

But selling cheap to get paid is your *last* resort, not a regular option, and if undertaken under duress it must be a prelude to getting out of a Latin American line of business altogether.

In fact, knowing that there is going to be this kind of pressure on you while waiting for your money suggests that you should be padding your prices beforehand to ensure that you are paid for being your partner's banker.

But price padding, of course, makes you less competitive, and there is plenty of competition around. You are thus likely to be inhibited from fully covering your risks and implicit credit costs.

One thing that must be obvious is that price-cutting to get business is a short-term strategy for trade with South America (or, for that matter, anywhere else). If you strip your prices by shaving your profit you end up with losses.

You are also likely to end up with losses if you only charge your normal rates when trading into administratively difficult places. Also, you are unlikely to make a worthwhile profit if you deal in small quantities of low-value items. Hence, don't.

Using somebody else's money

Trade with Latin America has to be in big-league quantities of goods and services, which probably means that you will be dealing with major trading partners (perhaps local subsidiaries of multinational companies) or with the country's government.

If the vagaries of getting paid by your importing partner worry you enough for you to seek business elsewhere, you might want to consider getting into the relatively secure business of trading with South American countries for money that belongs neither to you nor the country you are trading with.

Almost every day of every year, some development agency in the world approves economic aid to one developing country or another, and the benefits of access to these funds are sufficient inducement for South American governments to relish their countries being classed as 'developing'.

The benefit of a development grant lies in the fact that you get paid by the agency (the World Bank or whatever) for sending your products to the country concerned. You do not have to await the ponderous administrative procedures of the country's customs office or its financial institutions. If the World Bank grants you a contract to supply Argentina with your products you can take it that your bank account will be credited without any problems.

In fact, a quick sweep of the various development agencies that finance such deals, including the local field offices of these agencies located in South America, could provide you with your initial sales leads.

Aid agencies publish regular lists of tenders you can bid for, and personal contact on the spot could be the start of a useful relationship. Being seen in the country by people able to point you in the direction of government agencies looking to import your kind of products is better than sending them a letter even in flawless Spanish (or Portuguese), though that is better than waiting for them to contact you!

Getting your products to their attention may initiate the process by which the local office of the aid agency prompts the relevant department to get its government to approach the head office of the aid agency to finance a deal to buy your products. Sounds complicated but more than one multi-million-dollar deal has begun with a negotiator calling in at a local aid agency office and getting to know the guy behind the desk where the aid deals are first put together.

Finding an agent
Much of the international trade with Latin America that is not financed by world aid agencies or which does not involve direct dealings with the government or a state-owned company is promoted by some version of the agency system.

Some governments encourage foreign companies to set up manufacturing subsidiaries in partnership with nationals inside the country. They mainly do this by discouraging imports. Where this is not commercially suitable for your business — too small a local market, for instance — you have no alternative but to arrange to import your goods into the country. For this you will need a local agent.

You can try sending out your own resident representative, but even he will have to deal through a network of local agents or somebody who has, or claims to have, such a network working for him.

Your first negotiation in South America is likely to be with the national who desires (though he may not give you that impression by his demeanour) to be your officially appointed agent. Agents the world over come in two kinds: those that work for you all the time and those that work for you some of the time (if at all).

Care, of course, must be taken to select a good agent, but this is easier said than done. He might claim to have representatives in every corner of Brazil, and he can certainly produce expense claims that suggest he has an army of sub-agents working for him out of the best suites at the Rio Sheraton, but you need to check his claims thoroughly. You need coverage all over Brazil or at least Rio de

Janeiro, São Paulo and Minas Gerais (and, perhaps, the duty-free zone of Manaus).

Getting rid of a bad agent is not easy, and local laws exist in some, but thank goodness not all, South American countries to discourage the consequences of your outrage when you find him sitting on a warehouse full of your goods with not a paid invoice in sight.

Suing him in, say, Venezuela or Ecuador will cost you a small fortune, because his country's laws work for him and not for you, the foreigner. He's also likely to be entitled to compensation for your 'arbitrary' dismissal. (Remember, local courts the world over define almost any dismissal of one of their countrymen as arbitrary.)

On the other hand, in Uruguay you can sack an agent without risk of a damaging compensation dispute, but the stakes you are likely to be trading for in Uruguay compared to Venezuela are likely to be so small as to hardly make it worth the telex fee to sack him. In Peru, the law, surprisingly, supports you against the local agent.

To get the agent position sorted out — and you must do so in your own best interests — you will have to get into the field, perhaps putting one of your own people in residence (make sure he or she speaks Portuguese in Brazil and Spanish everywhere else), and negotiate good incentive terms that make the agent work for your products and not your rivals'. (Check that he is not an agent for all the leading brands in your field, if only to protect your negotiating flanks.)

Check out the local laws. For example, in Brazil you will be liable for Brazilian profits tax if officials assume that your agent can bind you to a deal he makes with a third party, while in Venezuela it has to be pretty clear that your agent is your representative.

Your negotiating objectives must be to make the contract specific about what your agent can and cannot do in your name and what entitlements he has to orders he generates himself and to those that come to you without his intervention.

Ideally, you want him tied to sales targets, with clear performance standards as a prelude to contract termination or renewal. Realistically, where there are more foreign vendors than local agents (as in Venezuela, for instance), you may simply be getting a deal that gets your products into his distribution system with no guarantees at all that he will push your interests among all his other obligations.

RUM DEALS IN THE POOL

A vice-president of a UK beer company was on a business tour of South America and was telexed by his head office to go to Jamaica on his way back and meet with the management team of one of the local rum exporters. His problem was that he did not have the work permit required for a business visit to Jamaica, nor on his tight schedule did he have time to acquire one.

Hence, he went into Norman Manley airport, Kingston, as a tourist. His problems began at immigration, because it was obvious from his previous itinerary and correspondence in his briefcase that he had been on a business trip. He claimed to the officials that he was in Jamaica for a few days' recreation before returning to London.

He booked into his hotel and phoned the rum exporter he wanted to meet. Later at the hotel he was interviewed by an immigration official who accused him of being in Jamaica for business purposes without a proper work permit. The official told him that he was being watched and that if he did any business at all he would be arrested, fined heavily and deported.

For two days a policeman shadowed him everywhere and forced him to spend the days and evenings like a tourist. The visit was clearly going to be a waste of time and money.

Before leaving, however, he met with the rum exporter and they did a deal right under the nose of the police.

The hotel has a patio bar, one side of which is built into the pool for swimmers to sit beside while in the water. While a policeman sat keeping a sleepy eye on him, he sat at the bar in the pool talking to the barman and a young woman who joined them.

The policeman assumed that he was merely idling his time talking to a barman and flirting with a guest. In fact he was negotiating with the head of the rum company who was behind the bar dressed as a barman. His secretary was the 'guest' undressed in a bikini in the pool.

Moral: Initiative can beat any bureaucratic nonsense aimed at stopping people doing business.

Business manners

The way business is conducted in a country reflects its social mores. This results in a manageable variation of business manners in South and Central America. Broadly, Latin America is a combination of Mediterranean and indigenous culture. There is very little that is naturally Northern European in their business culture. Typically, for example, it is said of the Argentinians that they are Italians who speak Spanish and think they are English.

Argentinians are certainly more formal than most of their continental neighbours. Buenos Aires (or 'BA' – as in 'LA' – to the resident English speakers) is a very European city, and shares with many European countries the habit of incessantly shaking hands at every opportunity. (Make sure you are ready to shake hands wherever you go in South America. It is an absolutely minimum symbol of good manners and respect.

Brazilians have a reputation for fun loving – the world-famous Copacabana beach is only one of several near Rio de Janeiro where the sensuous indulge their hedonism – and they wholly deserve what they enjoy. In business matters the Brazilian works on an inter-personal level. If he likes you he will do business with you, but even then he will not let business get in the way of his leisure. (So avoid trying to open negotiations during *Carnival* – for one thing the din is so loud you wouldn't hear what was being said!)

Chile, Paraguay, Uruguay and Colombia are very conservative places in which to do business. Politeness, including correct forms of address (and correct forms of dress), is mandatory. Don't turn up for negotiations wearing casual clothes. Stick to a business suit, lightweight if necessary, but conservative at all times.

In Peru they are positively Italian or Greek in their disregard for punctuality, and in Ecuador do not expect anybody to keep an appointment until you are actually shaking their hand (and even then you may be greeting an apologetic messenger). *Benign* persistence is required, particularly with government negotiators.

It is incumbent upon you, the foreigner, to make and confirm your appointments and to turn up on time for them. The vagueness about time-keeping is a characteristic reserved for the national concerned and you had better not 'go native' and indulge in it yourself just in case your opposite number takes offence at your insensitivity.

Finally, remember that while Central and South America have a great deal in common – the similarities they share – they are also extremely diverse and fiercely determined to leave it that way.

TIPS FOR TRAVELLERS IN SOUTH AMERICA

Thieves (and worse) are endemic in Belize City, Belize; Bogota, Colombia (the 'thieves' capital of the world') and in Georgetown, Guyana. It's also risky after dark in Kingston, Jamaica. In Panama City, Panama, avoid touts of anything. Daylight thieves abound in Mexico City, Mexico, but in Quito, Ecuador, they mainly work the night shift. Rio de Janeiro during *Carnival* is a wonderful social occasion but it can be dangerous; in 1985 ninety-six people were killed in four days of the world's longest samba.

Personal safety and security of property are more or less assured in Buenos Aires, Argentina (though always refer to the Falklands as the Malvinas); Montevideo, Uruguay (keep off politics altogether); and in Santiago, Chile (not a good place for political seminars).

Venezuela reveres Simon Bolivar, who liberated this and neighboring countries from the Spanish. Be extremely respectful about Bolivar statues and places named after him. It is useful to remember that in Caracas there are four rush hours for traffic, the usual two plus two more to accommodate the penchant of *caraquenos* for siesta. Venezuelan taxi drivers do not automatically accept a fare — they may haggle with you about whether they are going to take you at all (and they frequently get lost themselves in the jumbled unmarked streets of the city). Similarly, in Brazil assume the taxi driver is a total stranger in the city and get the hotel porter to give him precise directions.

Don't visit La Paz, Bolivia, if you have a respiratory or heart complaint. The high altitude (over 12,000 feet) is exhausting for a fit person and positively lethal for the rest of us. NB: La Paz is not the sort of city you go to for an *affaire de coeur,* unless it's a mutual suicide pact. Try Rio de Janeiro instead.

Brazilian visa regulations for business negotiators are notorious for their complexity; hence, go on a tourist visa. For other countries check with your travel agent.

If you refrain from interfering in their social structures, keep your views on how the world is best run to yourself (no comments are advisable on how local army squads might be going about their sometimes assertive business), and have the patience to learn about the pace of business in the country you are visiting, you will be well on your way to establishing the personal relationships essential for doing business with a Latin American.

Answers to self-assessment test 7

1 (a) Not if you want to do business with people who are somewhat sensitive to foreigners who lecture them on their past. (-10)

  (b) The wiser choice. It gets them talking about the subject: what makes their country tick and what doesn't, which they know more about than you do. And even if they are wrong, it's their history and they won't take kindly to you telling them otherwise. (10)

  (c) You are of a Kamikaze disposition! If you mention this in Mexico you deserve Montezuma's revenge. (-20)

  (d) Still an appalling arrogance on your part, especially if you detailed the reforms you thought were necessary. Stay off politics, history and reforms. (-15)

2 (a) While many Brazilians understand Spanish they seldom if ever speak it. They speak Portuguese instead and would think you irritating if you did not know the difference. (-10)

  (b) Better to speak English, even through an interpreter, than Spanish if you do not know (Brazilian) Portuguese. (10)

3 (a) His financial standing, while important, is not enough background on him and his business for you to sign a contract. This only tells you that he has financial resources; you want to know if he can market your goods. (-10)

  (b) It is essential that you find out if he is going to represent you exclusively, or you and your rivals. If he is serving your competitors too, what negotiating position do you think this puts him in? Moreover, does he have facilities outside Caracas to sell your products? (10)

Self-assessment test 8

1 You are visiting China for the first time in order to discuss with the National Machinery Import and Export Corporation (MACHIMPEX) the sale of heavy duty pumps and they inform you that China needs to replace 100,000 pumps over the next five years. They tell you that initially they want to buy five of your type of pumps (which you sell around the world for about $9000 each) and if your price is lower than your competitor's you could get the order. Do you:

(a) Go in at a price of $9000?

(b) Give them a large 'trial' discount to get your five pumps into China with a view to the follow-on orders for the 100,000 they need later?

(c) Quote a price per pump of $10,500?

2 You are negotiating with the China National Cereals, Oils and Foodstuffs Import and Export Corporation to import from China various traditional foodstuffs. What do you expect them to agree to in respect of payment:

(a) Payment in hard currency on your receipt of the goods?

(b) Payment in hard currency on the despatch of the goods?

(c) Payment in hard currency at a date to be agreed, loosely related to the actual despatch of the goods?

3 You are in the export–import business, and in Peking, the authorities offer you the use of letter of credit facilities to cover transactions with the Chinese Foreign Trade Corporations. These facilities allow for 'irrevocable, transferable and divisible' letters of credit through the Bank of China. Do you expect the same terms and obligations to apply for both exports (where they are the payers) and imports (where you are the payer)?

(a) Yes

(b) No

9 The scrutable Chinese

or, how they do business in Peking

Soviet style trade monopoly

The Chinese have based their foreign trade system on that of the Soviet Union – it is very Stalinist in scope and content. Much that has been discussed in Chapter 4 applies to the conduct of commercial negotiations with representatives of the People's Republic of China (PRC). Recent developments in China, combined with its divergence from the Soviet Union over the past twenty-five years, have produced variations in the Soviet-style system that are important and are more than mere nuances of emphasis. For a start, there is now greater scope for foreign businesses to negotiate trade deals with the Chinese state bureaucracy, and greater willingness on China's part, if it suits the current requirements of the Chinese economy, to seek out appropriate business deals with Western firms.

Much, however, remains familiar. Bureaucratic delays, endless reviews by a labyrinth of committees, hard bargaining on prices and performance guarantees, and the general (though sometimes genial) atmosphere of semi-suspicion at the motives of outsiders, characterize business negotiations with the PRC.

The purpose of China's monopoly of foreign trade system is similar to that of the Soviet Union: it is an instrument for maintaining the absolute leading role of the Communist Party in all aspects of the relationship of its citizens with the outside world. In addition, it has the economic effect of ensuring that trade does not interfere with the centralized state economic plan; citizens pursuing their own ventures with foreigners are incompatible with a planned economy.

The Foreign Trade Organization (FTO) handles everything in connection with the proposed business transaction and this, in the main, precludes direct contact between the foreign trader and the end-user of the product. Hence, the initial contact with the Chinese is likely to be indirect – you are approached, or approach, somebody acting for another party (who in turn need not be the end-user of your product, or, if you are buying, need not be the supplier).

The Chinese bureaucracy

If the deal is originated in China the process that they must go through before you are approached is complex, as well as methodical. The local plant, or industry committee, perceives a need for, say, machinery of a special kind. They will initiate discussions with the State Planning Commission which may consider acquiring the machinery from overseas. If so, it must pass the request through a procedure aimed at carefully scrutinizing the merits of the case for overseas acquisition (the potential benefits of China acquiring a new technology play a role here).

If the proposal survives this process (and, in view of the shortages of foreign exchange, the proposal competes with the others under consideration at that time), the Ministry of Foreign Trade will seek, through its overseas agencies, information on potential sellers of the machinery. It could invite overseas suppliers to address technical seminars in China (which might be your first contact with the Chinese as potential customers). There is, however, still a long way to go before the potential order for your products is turned into an actual order to take delivery of the goods, and you ought not to count your chickens etc., or indeed even think about them!

Again the two-stage negotiating process, familiar to Soviet traders, will be followed. One set of negotiations will take place on the technical aspects of the product, usually with somebody representing the end-user. Another set of negotiations will get under way regarding the commercial aspects of the deal, usually with representatives of the Ministry financing the exchange.

Even assuming that everything goes reasonably well in the, often, prolonged negotiations, the actual decision to initiate the purchase must still await bureaucratic approval from those whose task it is to operate and implement the state plans. What suits the Chinese agency that you have dealt with, let alone what suits you, does not necessarily carry the same weight with those whose horizons are bounded by other weighty matters, such as fitting the pressing demand for goods into an already elaborately conceived plan that must, on paper, balance requirements against resources.

Imports and exports in China are constrained by the country's overall economic targets, which include the availability of foreign currency to pay for imports. The Ministry of Foreign Trade is charged with responsibility for meeting import and export targets and is extremely reluctant to adapt its policies to meet new demands without prolonged consultation with all the overlapping bureaucratic interests who have, or are likely to have, a view about the decision or its implications.

There is no doubt that the Chinese bureaucracy is as cumbersome and as slow as any found in communist regimes. Its follies are partly based on the interests in self-preservation of the individual bureaucrats and partly on the functional interests of the system.

If a monopoly of foreign trade is a function laid down by the interests of preserving a communist economic and social system, then it behoves those charged with implementing the policy to exercise their monopolistic powers in the time-honoured way of all bureaucracies: with due care and attention to detail. In a word: slowly!

And you can take it that Chinese bureaucrats do precisely this and that they are not too worried about the inevitable delay this causes before they are in a position to make a decision to open negotiations with you (followed by further delays while they get confirmation of the negotiated deal you have agreed with them).

Making the first approach
Being a heavily centralized society, the Chinese that you deal with are more than likely based in Peking and it is in this ancient city that you will do most of your negotiating. Getting there in a physical sense is much easier than getting an invitation to go there.

You could try the unsolicited approach if you don't mind having to put up with being a 'tourist' rather than a business negotiator (and what better city to be a tourist in than Peking?), but on the whole the unsolicited trip, assuming that the Chinese grant you a visa for one, is likely to be a waste of your (business) time, as you are almost certainly never going to be able to sort out who to see, where to find them, and what influence they have in an uninvited trip of this nature.

Probably the best approach is to make contact with the relevant commercial section of the nearest Chinese embassy (and, please, make sure that you know the difference between the People's Republic of China and the Republic of China, otherwise you could

119

end up asking for a visa to Taiwan China instead of Peking China, and believe me there is a difference!).

You can offer them samples of your business literature, including detailed technical descriptions of your products. They will, in due course, forward these to the relevant ministry in Peking. If you know which ministry covers your products, or which Foreign Trade Corporation is responsible for importing your products, you can, of course, send your technical literature directly to them in China.

Whichever approach you use, you would be best advised not to expect an early reaction, and by 'early' I mean a response in anything much under a year. This is your first lesson in patience (there will be many more before you actually receive your first cheque from the Bank of China!) and you should learn it well.

Other ways of getting your products to the notice of Chinese negotiators include attendance at Trade Fairs in China or, if you belong to an appropriate organization, through visiting China as a member of a 'delegation' (perhaps your Chamber of Commerce or Trade Association). In this last respect, watch for trade visits to China sponsored by the government (in the United Kingdom, the British Overseas Trade Board organizes trade visits to almost everywhere, though on some of them the link between your product and the visit can be somewhat more than tenuous).

You can also arrange, at your own company's expense, to hold a technical seminar in Peking and, through this, demonstrate to interested Chinese bureaucrats your products and your technical competence. In fact their first response to your approach might very well be to offer such a facility to you, with you bearing your own costs and they in return rounding up myriads of their specialists to sit in on your demonstrations and talks.

If the Chinese approach you first – perhaps your product has come to their attention in a technical journal – you are obviously a little further down the negotiating track than if you make the first move, though I would not base your export programme to China on the basis that you wait for them to come to you first.

Technical negotiations
No matter how far down the track you start you will still need to go through the serious business of technical evaluation of your product, though you should remember while this is going on that these meetings are a part of, and not separate from, the negotiation.

HOW MUCH FOR ONE?

China does not have an indigenous civil aviation industry and in the 1960s purchased civil aircraft from both Britain (Tridents) and the USA (Boeings). These negotiations were long and arduous as the Chinese fought over every clause and for every cent.

Having got the aircraft delivered and in operation, they discovered that they did not have the equipment to move the aircraft about the tarmac and only one firm in the world supplied the necessary vehicles.

As the Chinese, for a change, were in a hurry, they telexed the US firm and asked them to quote a price for one of their vehicles. The US firm replied by telex with a price quote.

The next telex they received asked them to quote for twenty vehicles and demanded a quantity discount!

The US firm replied with a discounted price and received an order for delivery immediately.

The Chinese might have got a bigger discount if they had got a discounted price for ten vehicles in the first instance, followed by twenty, but even so they did all right as instant purchasers in the US market.

The technical negotiations can be exhausting and to the extent that you tire of them the more likely you will be to make concessions in a vain attempt to speed them up ('a decision, give me a decision, anything for a decision!').

Your response to a technical interrogation (and it could last for thirty or forty working days) ought to be a combination of great patience, respect for your Chinese opponents and an absolute determination to be prepared to bring the technical discussions to an end when clearly they are using them for improper (in the commercial sense) purposes.

The absent end-user
You may try, if you wish, to counter-interrogate the Chinese on the end-user of your product. You are unlikely to be offered much in the way of information about who will use your product, what they will use it for and what conditions they will use it in. This makes it a

trifle difficult to adjust your proposition to the needs of the user, which can be important in relation to the specifications that you agree to and the arrangements you make with them regarding maintenance, servicing, training and spare parts to be included in the deal.

It is easier to move mountains with one's bare hands than it is to get the Chinese to tell you much about the end-user. They live in a highly secretive society, distinctly compartmentalized, and operate a 'need to know' policy among themselves that is a model for a paranoid security organization.

Their unwillingness to discuss the end-user might also be due to the simple fact that they do not know the answers themselves, though evidence suggests that even if they do know the answers they regard it as none of your business and cannot see why or how this limits your ability to provide them with a tailor-made service.

Commercial negotiations

Once the commercial stage of the negotiations is entered, the Chinese will press for concessions on everything from price per unit, through finance for the deal, to delivery and the usual panoply of penalty clauses. Given that the technical aspects of the deal are dealt with first, it suggests that it is reasonable to withhold commitments on prices and finance until this stage is complete (and watch those commitments they want from you to include training their personnel in the package without charge).

In your eagerness to enter the Chinese market you might signal – even in writing! – price concessions from the start. If you do, you will regret your haste with even greater speed once they start talking about money.

The outlook of the Chinese buyer is clouded by his perceptions of your company as a member of the capitalist system, with you playing the unlikely role of a 'bourgeois' exploiter, ruthlessly playing the market to get fabulous and unjustified profits. He also knows that you live in a competitive environment – nominally alien to his experience of living under a state monopoly – and believes that his monopoly position (representing the 'workers and peasants of China') enables him to put competitive pressure on you.

Not having competition internally available to push you on price, the Chinese will quote external competition, perhaps from within your own country, and they are quite prepared to stage manage some 'capitalist' competition, or expose you to signs of some real competition that happens to be in town, in order to put elementary price pressure on you.

Now it is amazing, given the facts of life in capitalist societies where competition is a daily experience, that many Western negotiators price-crumble with alarming speed (not to say alacrity) when faced with price pressure from communist negotiators. Naturally, such behaviour by Western negotiators only encourages the Chinese to repeat the same demands to every visiting Western negotiator since it appears to be a successful way to provoke bouts of price-crumbling.

If Western negotiators, selling valuable products in China, see this market as one in which they must cut to the bone and beyond in the matter of prices, it little behoves the Chinese to teach them their business. The vulnerability of suppliers to versions of the 'sell cheap, get famous' gambit is legendary in Western economies but many who should know better seem totally helpless when the guy trying it on is wearing a 'Mao' suit and appears to be representing 900 million potential customers. The fact that going in with very low prices does not lead to massive future business ought to be a sufficient caution to you if you are ever tempted by the illusion that it does.

The use of competition

In the West most of us are familiar with the 'Dutch auction' technique of negotiating. Briefly, in a Dutch auction the price to be paid for an item is reduced successively until somebody calls out that they will buy it at that price. Naturally, the pressure is on the bidders, because whoever calls out first gets the item at whatever price the auctioneer has reached. They can remain silent and hope that nobody will call out at the last bid and thus force the auctioneer to try a lower price. If they get it wrong and a rival bids at the going price those who remained silent are automatically shut out of the bidding.

(The standard 'British' auction reverses this procedure. The auctioneer calls out successively higher bids, and bidders nod or signal their willingness to pay that price. When there is nobody else bidding the remaining bidder gets the item at whatever price the auctioneer last called.)

The Chinese often play off rivals for their business in a version of a 'Dutch auction'. Here, they will take your price offers as they are presented and disclose them to your rivals, who may even be in the next room (I have heard of one negotiation in Canton where the rivals were seated at adjacent tables and able to hear directly what each said as the Chinese negotiators moved openly between them!).

Your rival has the opportunity to match or better your offer. If you find this reprehensible, remember you will almost certainly be given the opportunity to respond to your rival's bid. It is a test of your nerve not to be drawn into such a game. The general effect is, of course, that Western negotiators have their prices forced down, sometimes below the point of profitability.

You will be told by the Chinese negotiator that you have lots of competition. They may not believe in competition for ideological reasons, but do not let that fool you: they think they know how to make competition work in the national interests of China, and this generally consists of acting the part of the aggressive buyer waiting for you and your rivals to maul each other's prices.

For obvious reasons, you are a long way from home when you are negotiating in Peking. You are likely to have spent some considerable time in the negotiations before you reach the question of price. By pressurizing you into believing that the world and his aunt are in the next room ready to sign the deal you have spent months trying to put together, they hope you will crumble and give it to them even cheaper, rather than pack your bags and go home empty-handed.

The remedy is in your hands: don't price-crumble because they tell you about, or even show you in the flesh, the competition. Tie your deal together with conditional propositions; link every element of it together to prevent them from picking off concessions on an item by item basis; and, above all, insist that if they alter the terms of one item in the deal you must make a corresponding adjustment in another item. If you do not use some version of the above advice you will end up being Dutch auctioned into numerous concessions.

Pad your prices

Another protection for your prices is to anticipate price pressure from the start and to pad them beforehand. Failure to do this, in a misguided effort to look price competitive against real and imaginary competition, can leave you short when you collect on your invoices.

You should bear in mind that the only reason that you are even talking to the Chinese about a potential deal is because they, or rather somebody else in the labyrinthian Chinese bureaucracy, has decided that they need the type of product that you are so anxious to sell to them (or, if they are exporting, they need the earnings that they will get from selling their products to you).

This means that you are not in a casual or opportunistic negotiating relationship with the Chinese; if you see them across the table from you then you can take it that somebody somewhere in their country wants to do business with you if you can supply them with what they are ordered to acquire.

Anticipating price pressures is particularly important in the matter of the negotiations on how the deal is to be financed. 'Who gets how much of the money and when do they get it' is not an idle question. They may be communists dedicated to the proposition that capitalist finance is robbery but they sure know how to squeeze careless capitalists who forget to cover themselves against financial payment routines designed to provide their customers with free credit.

Letters of credit

The Chinese pay for their exports and imports using the letter of credit system. The demand for foreign currency is so high in the spending plans of the Chinese Foreign Trade Corporations that they cannot pay for everything they wish to purchase by means of foreign (hard) currency reserves. Hence, they use the letter of credit system to ease their foreign exchange problems at the expense of foreign traders who make unwarranted assumptions about when cash and goods are supposed to change hands.

The Chinese operate their foreign trade using contracts that they have drawn up beforehand, and they rigidly refuse to allow amendments to these pre-printed contracts, especially when the amendments are designed to suit the interests of the foreign trader.

When they are exporting Chinese produce they require that the foreign purchaser opens a 'confirmed, irrevocable, transferable and divisible' letter of credit in favour of the seller (i.e. China) at a branch or approved agent of the Bank of China. The phraseology is important: the fact that it is *confirmed* means that the importer's bank guarantees payment as long as the documentation meets the terms of the contract; it is *irrevocable* in order to prevent an importer withholding payment for any reason whatsoever, including the condition of the goods when they arrive (a singularly blanket condition which they do not reciprocate with respect to

125

THE SHIFTING CHINESE MIDDLE

A European firm, world-renowned in the oil industry, was asked by the Chinese to enter into negotiations to supply their services to the small but growing domestic Chinese off-shore oil industry.

The Chinese, who are anxious to develop their oil resources and are using Western technology to do so, went hard at the prices quoted by the European firm.

First, they got a price quotation for the company supplying its services for three years, then they demanded inclusive of the quoted price a lot of extras.

Among these extras were some very expensive add-ons, such as free training for Chinese nationals, free manuals for operating the specialized equipment, masses of spares and stores, and domestic charges for accommodating the company's technical staff. This last was a trifle ambitious on the part of the Chinese who insisted that the foreign staff be charged at the same *per diem* rate for subsistence that they were charged for their staff visiting Europe where prices and living standards are, of course, much higher.

The European negotiators fought hard to avoid pricing themselves into unprofitability and regularly complained that when they made a concession the result was not a reciprocal move on the part of the Chinese. Far from it. The Chinese regarded 'split the difference' moves as invitations to put pressure on the Europeans to move even closer to the Chinese opening position.

The remedy was in the Europeans' hands: pad their prices before they opened negotiations; never make a single concession without getting something back from the Chinese; avoid any 'fair play' illusions about 'split the difference' gambits; totally resist the 'add-on' ploys; and, lastly, sit it out, for the Chinese need oil technology far more than oil technologists need to work in China.

their own exports); it is *transferable* to enable the Bank of China to use it directly to pay for other transactions; and it is *divisible* to give flexibility in using it for part payments.

The letter of credit comes into operation up to thirty days before the Chinese agency is due to ship the goods *towards* the importer (i.e. in some cases this could literally mean the ex-works shipment date and not the sailing date at the Chinese port).

If the actual date of shipment is delayed (and delays of some months are not unknown in China) this means effectively that the importer has paid for the goods before having sight of them, which means he has unwittingly gotten into the lending-money-at-no-charge business, which is a sure fire way to go bankrupt.

The only thing that the importer might have had sight of is the draft on his bank requiring it to pay to the Bank of China the full import price of the goods. You can see why you have to be careful here in accepting stringent terms in the letter of credit! If you don't, you had better do a crash course in banking. Your credit control people might have views about your negotiating skills if you accept contract terms that turn you into an international moneylender instead of an importer of soya sauce.

Having lent the Chinese government considerable sums of money, no doubt you will come to be regarded by the Chinese as a great friend of China and, if you are rich enough to afford this privilege, good luck to you. If you aren't, then you had better build into your purchase prices some amount to cover the interest you are effectively having to forgo to permit them to borrow from you. From the Chinese point of view, the use of free credit of this nature enables them to use your money to finance their other transactions and it is good business for them to be in. With annual exports worth over $500 million, the savings in interest they gain by using free credit is quite considerable.

When it comes to imports into China, a similar letter of credit system operates and it has the same characteristic of being designed to benefit the People's Republic of China rather than the supplier. China makes its payments for its imports by letters of credit issued to suppliers that are payable *only* at the Bank of China (thus curtailing separate trading in Chinese letters of credit in international markets). These letters of credit are also irrevocable, transferable and divisible, though they are not confirmed (which has the effect of enabling the Bank of China to withhold payments from you in certain cases). Neither are they truly irrevocable as described above: all imports into China are subject to their own state inspection, and payment is only authorized when imports meet Chinese government standards and their interpretation of the contract.

To get payment after a shipment has been despatched you will have to send your documents of proof to Peking. From this moment on you have no control over the transaction as you have let your products and the original documents for payment out of your sight. Your commercial interests are now truly at the mercy of the People's Republic of China.

It can take time to get your payments processed at the Bank of China in Peking. Every day's delay is an interest free loan to the Chinese government. If you try to circumvent this by getting a bank in your own country to pay you on account, while the Bank of China wades through its own procedures, it will cost you what the local bank charges for discounting your invoices. You ought, therefore, to reflect your generosity as a lender of currency to the Chinese and as a discountee to your local bank in your pricing policies. In other words, your prices must reflect the true costs to you of doing business with the Chinese, otherwise you will end up too poor to do business with them.

Contract negotiations

The crunch is going to come when you are negotiating the commercial contract. The Chinese share with the Japanese an aversion to legalistic language, particularly where it is confusing or obscure. They do not share the Japanese aversion to detail in their contracts, following in this respect a more Stalinist model of contract design. One contract with China worth $125 million had a page in it for every million dollars and it covered every conceivable eventuality. It, like most other Chinese contracts, was unashamedly biased in favour of them rather than the supplier.

If you can get a straightforward sales or purchase contract without complications and conditions, you can consider yourself very lucky. In this you get paid or pay when the goods are shipped (subject to whatever concessions they have squeezed out of you regarding finance through their letters of credit). The Chinese, like the Soviets and other soft currency countries, have expanded the role of barter in their international trading, and earlier remarks on this subject apply.

128

Barter trade

China trades with 167 countries and has over 80 bilateral trading agreements in operation. Some proportion of this trade can be paid for in hard currency earnings, some through extended credit deals with Western banks. Both means of payment have constraints. Hard foreign currency has to be earned, normally from hard currency countries and it is not always the case that the recipients of China's trade have sufficient foreign currency holdings themselves (for example, Third World clients are short of hard currency too). With extended credit from world banks, the obvious problem is the debt-servicing requirements that can alarm a developing country faced with massive and growing overseas borrowings.

Barter trade can be attractive in these circumstances. China can contract to use its abundant and relatively cheap labour to process, or part process, raw materials supplied by foreign traders and to re-export them to the supplier for world-wide distribution. The supplier might even supply the machinery too, and China could receive its fees for doing this in the form of some proportion of the output of the plant.

This system can enable the Chinese to acquire machinery and equipment not otherwise available to it. It is to be expected that when the Chinese territories adjacent to Hong Kong are in full operation as manufacturing and processing areas, this form of barter contract will become even more significant.

It takes time

In summary, negotiating with the Chinese authorities is bound to entail considerable time commitments on the part of Western companies, and the negotiations will follow the Soviet two-stage model of technical negotiations first, followed by commercial negotiations afterwards.

You will deal with one of the Foreign Trade Corporations acting on behalf of the end-user in respect of the product and on behalf of the Finance Ministry in respect of the finance for the deal. The composition of the Chinese negotiating teams will vary depending on the subject under discussion, and most times your opposite number will not have authority to make a settlement without consultation upwards into the Chinese bureaucracy.

They will need time to consider whether to import your product in its entirety or to import those parts of it that they cannot

CHINESE BARTER DEALS

The Chinese have gone into bartering in a big way, largely because their foreign trade requirements have expanded faster than their ability to finance them with hard currency earnings.

Some barter transactions have been a trifle bizarre, such as when an Australian company in 1979 traded six 200-room prefabricated hotels for large quantities of frozen and canned food!

Most deals tend to be related in some way. For instance, for setting up shrimp farms the supplier gets paid in supplies of shrimps. Similar deals occur with oil pipelines being paid for with supplies of oil, chemical plants with output of chemicals, light bulb plants with supplies of light bulbs, television plants with televisions, shipping container plants with shipping containers and so on.

manufacture themselves (this latter is important when the subject of spares is being discussed).

Their financial interests are influenced by their shortage of foreign currency and they will therefore be more likely to attempt to finance the deal using the letter of credit system. The pitfalls in this system from your point of view are summed up in the warning that you may unwittingly and unintentionally end up a lender to the Chinese government (the guy sitting next to you on the flight to Peking could be financing your deal through his badly negotiated letter of credit; conversely, you may be about to negotiate a deal that gives the Chinese sufficient free credit to pay for his deal!).

The Chinese appear to be awakening to the vast opportunities for trade with the rest of the world, and they are slowly abandoning the fallacy that they can 'leap forward' from relative economic backwardness to industrialized prosperity entirely by themselves. But they have a long way to go and could very easily falter or be forced to retreat, depending on political developments within the leadership of the Communist Party.

If you have something to sell them that they want badly enough to talk to you at all, you ought to bear this in mind when they try on well established 'capitalist' ploys to persuade or frighten you into

TIPS FOR TRAVELLERS IN CHINA

Chinese people have conflicting attitudes to things foreign. They know that they need foreigners to help them develop economically, and at the same time they resent their dependence as an affront to China's dignitiy. Be prepared for bouts of xenophobia, followed by incredible and touching displays of kindness.

In 1979 China adopted its own version of a romanized script for its characters. Out went 'Peking' and in came 'Beijing'; Canton became Guangzhou and Mao Tse-tung became Mao Zedong, etc. It is customary to use the local name when abroad, though permissible to use your own country's versions when at home. In Peking *always* refer to Beijing, likewise in Canton, and only refer to Mao when your hosts mention him, as he may be 'in' or 'out' of political favour at the time! Do not mention the Great Leap Forward, the Cultural Revolution, Madame Mao or Formosa.

It's cold in Peking from November to March, so dress accordingly. In Shanghai and Canton it's generally warm. Central heating and air conditioning are not common anywhere, hence dress warmer and cooler to suit than you would if you were visiting Japan or the USA.

Chinese business work from 8 a.m. to 6 p.m., six days a week. You get Sundays off, though shops open every day. Visitors can shop in 'Friendship Stores', which carry limited quantities of imports.

Hotel accommodation is scarce. Your hosts will arrange rooms or suites for you – do not expect advance warning of where you are staying. Guest houses are an alternative if you are part of a large party (but make sure meals are included). If you book a taxi (you cannot hail one in the street), keep it for the day. Once you give it up you may never see it again!

Do not tip anyone with cash. It's 'illegal'. Discreet gifts to the hotel for distribution to staff are acceptable. Do not make any sexual advances to anybody – the Chinese are very prudish.

Be ready for regular toasts during a meal. Always reciprocate ('to the friendship of our peoples' is a good stand-by, if stuck).

> Do not take photographs that include airfields, bridges, docks or public buildings in them. Also avoid cute children and elderly people as subjects, unless you ask them first.
>
> Everything you take into China must be accounted for before you leave. All Chinese money must be left behind.

giving them your products at 'take away' prices. You can bet yourself a bowl of fried rice to a chicken chop suey that though they are (presently?) of a communistic disposition they can teach a lot of capitalistic managers a thing or two about commercial negotiating.

If you have any doubts on this score you should consider just how good the overseas Chinese are at doing business as fully fledged capitalists, and you can take it from me that the Chinese still in China have not lost their touch when it comes to the haggle!

Answers to self-assessment test 8

1 *(a)* You are risking a heavy price squeeze from the Chinese which will put your profits under pressure or even eliminate them.   (-10)

   (b) No! Never go for the sell-cheap-get-famous fallacy. The Chinese use the fact of their large potential market as a lever to tempt your prices down, but remember that the Chinese market is only a potential one and not yet a reality (it is a very poor country) and anyway they have no intention of becoming dependent on the West for key resources such as engineering products.   (-15)

   (c) Much the best move. Always pad your prices when opening negotiations in a new and untried market. The Chinese will expect you to do so and will be very disappointed, to the point of disbelief, if you try to hold your prices in the face of demands for discounts etc.   (10)

2 *(a)* You are optimistic that they will allow their goods out of their sight without payment from you in their hands. To do this exposes them to the entire risk of the transaction and anyway they need the money sooner rather than later.

                                                                         (-10)

   (b) Logic and fair play says yes, but practice is different. The people responsible for despatching the goods are not the

132

same as those responsible for receiving the money, and the latter guys are very cautious about risks. (-5)

(c) Chinese sales contracts specify a payment date of up to thirty days before the despatch date. Bear in mind that the Chinese version of a despatch date is usually in the form of 'November-December 1986' and not a specific day in the year. You would therefore (in this example) pay for the goods on 1 September 1986 and could receive them anytime up to, say, February 1987, allowing for the sailing time and the usual delays. (10)

3 (a) No! You are clearly an honourable trader but the Chinese do not see things your way. While you, as an importer, will be required to open an irrevocable letter of credit in their favour (see question 2), you will not be permitted by its terms to revoke payment *for any reason* whatsoever; however, their obligations to pay you by an irrevocable credit for your exports to them is qualified by their right to inspect the goods on arrival in China. They can do this because the Chinese put all their transactions through the state Bank of China and they hold all the aces when it comes to payments. (-10)

(b) Yes! You will not be caught napping in China – though I doubt whether you will be able to avoid the usual risks of doing business with them. Some consolation: the Chinese are very good at paying what they agree to when they agreed to do so; there are very few cases of disputes and even fewer of default. (10)

Self-assessment test 9

1 You are selling highly specialized steels to a German company which agrees to proceed to contract, but just before signing they tell you that they must get a ten per cent price cut if the order is to go ahead. Do you:
   (a) Say no?
   (b) Say yes?
   (c) Agree if, and only if, your prices are free on board (FOB) instead of cost insurance and freight (CIF)?

2 You discover accidentally that your Swedish customer has been marking up your products by 800 per cent while squeezing your prices under threat of stiff competition from your rivals. Do you:
   (a) Confront them with what you have discovered and demand a price rise?
   (b) Save your information until the next price negotiation?
   (c) Ask them casually for details of their local pricing policy without disclosing what you know?
   (d) Say nothing because what they pay you is profitable anyway?

3 You are negotiating to buy a propulsion system from a British manufacturer. What is likely to be the most difficult thing to agree upon?
   (a) Price?
   (b) Finance?
   (c) Delivery?
   (d) Quality?

10   The European tribes

*or, negotiating with people
divided by a common future*

Old enmities

Europeans do a lot of business with each other. They used to spend
as much time fighting, thinking about fighting, or resting between
fights. Apart from the bloodshed, little has changed. Now they fight
over beef, lamb and fish quotas, imports, taxes, grants, funds and
economic policies. Those who thought that the European
Economic Community (EEC) was going to quickly change the
nature of the European peoples obviously got it all wrong. The EEC
hasn't changed them at all – at least not yet – it has only given their
eternal conflicts a new dimension to be played in.

Not that this is something to complain about. Better that
Germany and Britain argue over a couple of dozen cheap flights for
civil passengers between their cities than that their talented peoples
spend hours planning to send bombers over their respective
populations; better that France is flooded with cheap Italian wine
than that Italy is overrun by the descendants of Napoleon.

The history of Europe clearly has deeply influenced relationships
between all of its peoples. Though the last European war (called
Hitler's war nowadays, as if we wish to disown shared responsibility
for it) ended forty years ago, it still influences the attitudes of
ordinary people, though less so the attitudes of the young (always
defined as anybody less than half our own age).

Old enmities die hard but there is hope: the popular British press
loves to 'hate' the French for their insistence on arranging
European affairs to suit French national interests. Yesterday's allies
(known semi-affectionately as 'Frogs') against the 'Hun' have been
re-cast as the major source of British frustration in all matters
pertaining to the EEC and its budgets.

If the normally staid British can switch sides so dramatically –
assuming it is not just another manifestation of European inter-

tribal warfare with allies and enemies switching roles at the drop of a Franc or a Deutschmark – it suggests, perhaps, that the enmities are not too serious.

In Britain we take our enmities more seriously. I know people called MacDonald who still will not speak to a Campbell, or enter a place of business owned by a Campbell, and it makes not one whit of a difference whether they know or need them or not, so deep is the massacre of MacDonalds by Campbells at Glencoe in 1692 buried in MacDonald folklore.

In Northern Ireland, however, the Irish of the two communities continue to fight out their ancient enmities with a ferocity totally outside the understanding of outsiders. One side marches to tunes praising a King 'Billy' of 1690 while the other has memories of martyrs and massacres going back to Cromwell's time.

The rivalry between England and Scotland is an altogether less serious business, and thankfully it is largely confined to the exertions of twenty-two men on a soccer field once a year.

From the Atlantic to the Urals

Europe is a divided land. Geographically, according to the great French patriot, Charles De Gaulle, it stretches variously from the Atlantic to the Urals and from beyond the Arctic Circle to the Mediterranean. Politically it is divided into East and West by the so-called iron curtain; it is also divided into North and South by the weather – rain, snow, cold winds and odd spells of sunshine to the north; sunshine, hot climes and occasional rain to the south.

It is, or rather could be, the world's largest economic power, though its very real divisions preclude such an eventuality in the short term. If it was a united federation of states it would certainly be *the* dominant force in the world in almost all spheres, political, economic, technological and military.

The division of Europe into separate states, each with a national language and all the other trappings of statehood, is the great fact that must be faced in all its complexity and consequences. It is the divisions that determine the business culture (as much as the other kind of culture) and it is these that negotiators must come to terms with when contemplating engaging in trade across Europe's frontiers. And trade within Europe is rapidly growing, as it was meant to do under the EEC. The EEC countries are now Britain's largest trading partner, and there is no sign that inter-European trade is anywhere near saturation point. So, if you are in the international trade business at all, it is more than likely that you will be negotiating with your opposite number in one or more of the European states before long.

There is a considerable range of business behaviour in Europe, much of it conforming to national stereotypes, though you must be careful to allow for changing trends and tastes, as the integrative influences of increasing trade and contact between the nations are clearly wearing down national distinctions. Particularly under the influence of mass culture (or, to be frank, modern pop culture of the post-war generations), the safe stereotypes are looking more fragile than most people thirty or forty years ago would have thought likely. Particularly among the youth it is most difficult to tell one nation from another, until, that is, they start speaking.

Nevertheless, the distinctions, if a trifle blurred, are still recognizable and you will not go too far wrong by paying them some attention; at the worst, you will appear a little dated when you act as if they still exist in their full flower and glory.

The Germans

We can begin with the Germans. They represent the modern Europe in two distinct ways: first, they are divided into East and West by the very real border that separates the Federal German Republic of the West from the German Democratic Republic (GDR) of the East; second, both zones have the highest living standards and most advanced economies of their respective allies.

For the purposes of this chapter, following common usage, I shall refer to the Federal German Republic as Germany, and while much of what is said about Germany can also be applied to the GDR you ought to bear in mind that the economic and political system in the GDR qualifies the actual operation of their business culture, Germanic as the GDR may be overall. (I was once told by a Polish communist that the reason why the East Germans were so successful had more to do with the fact that they were Germans than the fact that they were also communists.)

The Germans have a well-deserved reputation for efficiency. They are capable of immense technical ingenuity and are extremely persistent in pursuit of their goals. An example from Hitler's war is apposite here. Despite four years of intense allied bombing of German industrial targets, they were producing more aircraft, tanks, artillery pieces and small arms in the Spring of 1944 than at any previous time since 1939 (fortunately, it was not enough to win the war, and in this sense allied bombing was 'successful').

Their industries operate to exacting technical standards and they expect the highest quality in the products that they buy or sell. If you are going to do business with the Germans you will have to convince them that your company can meet consistent standards in all aspects of the deal, and to some extent the way that they perceive your performance in the negotiations will determine how convincing you are about your commitments in this respect.

They certainly will approach the negotiations with a thoroughly professional preparation. This will extend not just to the product that you have come to buy or sell; it will also include a thorough research of your company as a potential business partner.

They will want to know, for example, just how financially sound your company is and how your proposition reflects that soundness. In financial matters they are extremely conservative and are risk averse. In their own business affairs they have relied on their banks for much of their finance (unlike the British they do not rely on a securities market to raise business finance), and banks the world over being bastions of caution and timidity, you will find the Germans ultra-cautious about propositions that leave them exposed to high risk of losses.

Germany functions because of its economic strengths – a sound currency (which constitutionally is under the control of the Federal Bank not the Bonn government) is one manifestation of its strength, a highly productive workforce is another – and these strengths are not based on highly opportunistic investments. The Germans invest in sound projects, using sound finance, with sound prospects of getting a profitable return, and they choose to work with companies abroad if they have something to offer which cannot be acquired locally and if they are unlikely to jeopardize the commercial strengths.

The German preference for local purchases is not purely nationalistic (as it is in France, for example). The integrity of a local company is more susceptible to close scrutiny than is the case with an overseas company. A German company has a local reputation and if it passes the usual tests it is more likely to get the business than a company outside Germany. But Germany does not have a monopoly in all aspects of technology and all products.

They will buy from foreigners if the foreigner has technological or

138

other advantages that cannot be found in Germany, and if the foreigner can deliver the products at the high standards the Germans require.

So you can expect to be given a hard time proving to them that your company's products meet their requirements. Do not, however, assume that you can easily exploit the scarcity value of your unique product in the face of a clear wish of the Germans to acquire it. They may very well be anxious to buy your product but you would not think so from the way they set about negotiating the commercial side of the deal.

The Germans are very good at commercial negotiating. They seem to be able to squeeze concessions out of nowhere once they decide to buy. They will put pressure on your delivery dates (especially if you are from Britain which is notorious all over Europe for lack of performance when it comes to delivery), arguing that they have to be assured of strict adherence to delivery promises to meet their own highly disciplined production schedules.

You could find yourself agreeing to a tight penalty clause on top of an even tighter delivery promise in order to get the business. To cover themselves they may even demand a generous (to them) warranty period for the performance of your product, plus extensive credit in anticipated compensation for you failing to meet them on this.

In fact, given the pleasant nature of the surroundings where you are likely to be negotiating with them – a lovely room with a panoramic view across green fields to the mountains – you might find yourself agreeing to all kinds of things. There are a lot of worse places on earth to visit each year to re-negotiate your deals!

The German is a hard bargainer. No matter how well you are established in your own country, it is likely that they will ask you for business references and, where possible, for a demonstration of your product in action either in your own plant or, preferably, in the plant of a current customer. They will want to talk to your technical people and to your customers, and all this before they have got to the subject of price.

Germany is a competitive environment to do business in and they will use this fact to put pressure on your prices. As they are doing business with you because they cannot get your product locally (at present), they will use the prospect of local competition to challenge your commercial proposals. The competition is real and your presence in the market could be temporary, and, when combined,

SIBERIAN GAS – WORST DEAL OF THE CENTURY?

From 1984 Siberian natural gas will flow 3600 miles to Western Europe, thanks to a $15 billion engineering feat of Western technology – and $10 billion of European capital.

Nothing illustrates the politico-commercial skills of the Soviet Union better than the details of this deal. Their ability to get the highly talented Europeans to put up the capital, take most of the risks, and this for only about 20 per cent of the gas (the rest being diverted into Soviet uses), is a remarkable testimony either to their negotiating prowess or to the negotiating errors of the Europeans.

How did the Soviets manage to pull of this coup? Simply by dividing the Germans, French, British, and Italians from each other. (They even managed to put one over on the Japanese, itself no mean feat.)

The Soviet negotiators went on tour from European company to European company, from German bank to French bank and then back again, each time picking up a concession here and a concession there. With their rivals making concessions, the Europeans responded with even greater concessions, to which inevitably the rivals responded too. Instead of treating the deal with a single monopolist customer as requiring a single European seller, the Western capitalist firms and their governments caved in one by one like lambs on their way to market.

The Dutch, with great credit to themselves, refused to play the Soviet game of 'Dutch auction' and tried to get collaboration across the interested parties. The Soviet response was open and brutal – they cut the Dutch out of the deal and went on to tackle the rest on a one by one basis.

these factors will cause you to draw on depths of resolve not to crumble.

To get into the German market you will have to be good at whatever it is that you do, and to stay in the market you will have to stay ahead in a technical sense. Above all, you must reach and maintain high quality standards. Otherwise, you will find your technology being acquired and improved upon by a rival who speaks the same language as your current German customer.

What was the deal? Basically, that Western countries would finance the project, provide the necessary technology and enter into purchase contracts at fixed prices for some of the gas.

The loans given to the Soviet Union were charged at a below market rate of 7 to 8 per cent (interest rates currently running at 11 per cent and over). The gas is to be purchased on twenty-five year contracts at prices tied to a one-way oil-price index (nice one, Ivan!). That is, if the world oil-price index rises, the Europeans pay more for their gas, if it falls below a certain level they still pay a fixed minimum price ($5.70 per million BTUs – compared to current Algerian gas prices of around $4.15) irrespective of how far the oil price index falls. If oil prices fall from $34 a barrel (when the deal was signed) to anything near $24 a barrel, the German, French and Italian consumers are going to look profligate in respect of the price their governments pay the Soviets for gas, and the Soviets are going to reap a windfall in hard currency.

The basic lesson is obvious: European negotiators must not deal with the Soviet Union separately on such massive joint projects. The governments, concerned as they inevitably have to be with national unemployment, must not allow themselves to be persuaded to underwrite national companies that follow kamikaze price policies to get international business. Above all, the bottom line in any negotiation with the Soviet government must be that if they want to use European capital for their projects they will have to pay the market rate like everybody else does.

In their personal relations German negotiators are formal and they expect you to be also. Until and unless you know your German opposite number very well, you should always refer to him as 'Herr Schmidt' rather than 'Fritz' (or as 'Doktor Schmidt', if appropriate). Formality extends to dress too and so get used to wearing a suit at almost all times (denims are *out*, unless you are selling to the 'alternative' youth society, in which case make sure that you do cash-only deals!).

The German disgust (there is no other word for it) at British unreliability in the matter of deliveries is likely to be brought to a frosty surface if you are late for a business appointment. So get there on time (and remember they start work earlier than is usual in the UK).

The one thing you won't have to worry about is getting paid, provided you meet the terms of your contract; conversely, they don't like to be kept waiting for their money. They are punctilious in their business affairs, formal in their relationships, and genuinely competitive in their outlook.

The French

The French have the reputation of being the most highly patriotic people in Europe but this could be misleading. The French government is extremely patriotic, it being its job to represent the best interests of France in all matters, and business organizations tend to operate in the same way. But not all French citizens are as deeply attached to the centralized French state as the organizations you are likely to be doing business with, and it is therefore sensible to refrain from making assumptions about the nationalistic attitudes of those you negotiate with until you are sure that you are not dealing with a disaffected Breton, a southerner or a Corsican.

It is true, however, that the French state works for France. It does not operate on behalf of foreigners, and if you come into contact with its representatives you should try not to behave as if you think its officials should pay attention to your interests (this is particularly true when dealing with policemen, customs officials, government clerks and politicians!).

If you negotiate with the French it is more than likely that the negotiations will take place in the French language, even if the French negotiator speaks perfect English. They seldom make any concessions on this, unless they happen to be abroad and need your business badly. So if a French negotiator speaks to you in English you have probably received the biggest concession you are likely to get that day.

They are distant rather than formal, though they have a habit of shaking hands more times than you expect to wash them in a day. I have been introduced to a French company's staff – all twenty-eight of them – with a handshake when I entered the room and with another one – from each of them again – when I left it. They do the same in cafés and bars.

It is always a good policy to turn up on time, no matter where you are in the world, but do not expect too much of the French in this respect. Sometimes they do and sometimes they don't and they have a ready run of plausible excuses – 'the traffic' is the most common – for being late. If you are late, for any reason, you will be received cooly, if they receive you at all, and they will only still be waiting for you if they need you (your second concession of the day?).

In social matters, such as a formal dinner, there is an informal convention that the more important the chief guest the later he or she will turn up – so if you are invited to a dinner with the company president you can expect to start eating about thirty minutes after the due time; with a cabinet minister it will take at least fifty minutes for him to get there; hence if you get hungry early eat with people of your own status or eat something beforehand if invited to a function.

The French have no compunction about taking advantage of you in a negotiation if they have the economic leverage to do so. They will hold you strictly to the deal and nothing but the deal for as long as it suits them. If it doesn't they will breach the deal and defy you to stop them.

Precedents exist for this odd behaviour. The government always acts in the national interest irrespective of what the EEC or anybody else says. If they don't want to receive Japanese exports they will introduce non-tariff barriers of the most blatant kind, such as requiring each and every item to be individually inspected at an obscure customs hall in the middle of rural France. The informal (and illegal) treatment of cheap Italian wine imports, or British lamb, is well known and more or less tolerated by the authorities.

Hence, you must examine the contract carefully. If you make concessions to get the business and accept some of the penalties they will endeavour to introduce, then you know what you will be in for if circumstances arise to occasion the penalties. This can lead to acrimonious relationships which will mainly feature the French sitting on their hands if they are in the wrong, or suing you if they think you are.

Relationships with the French must be entered into on a long-term basis before you get that 'normality' of goodwill common to relationships with others. If you can establish a good rapport with a French company over many years and can trade to mutual advantage without the blessing of accidental upsets, then you will find them extremely compatible partners. They might even warm to you socially and the pay-off that follows in terms of good food, great wine and lovely weather will make the 'atrocities' of the past well worth enduring.

The Italians

If the French can be exasperating in the punctuality with which they sometimes attend to formal dinners, the Italians are by far the least punctual people in Europe (the Arabs, however, deserve a place in the Guinness Book of Records for lack of punctuality, though I hear that some South Americans are even more lax). That is assuming that they turn up at all. I learned the hard way to check beforehand by telephone that a carefully arranged meeting was still scheduled – and even then on occasion found it had been unilaterally postponed during the time it took me to cross town by taxi!

Italian business leaders are frightfully autocratic when it comes to dealing with subordinates within their own organization and not much more 'democratic' when dealing with outsiders. Their organizations relish in protocol and status and they never accept an insult lying down. They are, however, *always* extremely charming about everything they do, even when telling you 'no' or *even* when telling you something more direct to do with yourself.

The Italians have a volatile temperament. One minute they are as high as a kite and the next as low as a client for the Samaritans. They gesticulate wildly, their shoulders, arms and hands convulsing in tempo with their voices. It can be a spectacle just to watch them making a point, hopefully in good humour, because if they are angry the performance is on the verge of hysteria. (If you see two Italians apparently about to come to blows do not intervene, they could just be arguing about whose turn it is to pay for the taxi.)

Italians love style, in fact they live by it ('bella figura' is no small part of their view of the world). Business negotiators tend to dress smartly, groom themselves neatly and occupy modern well-equipped offices. They make entrances and exits with a flourish, eat and drink well (but not excessively) and talk about their families with pride.

They are more informal than Germans and less distant than the French, though they are often impersonal in business matters. They take their time to make a decision, not, like the Chinese or Japanese, because they are consulting with colleagues, but out of a desire not to commit themselves too quickly. If you are on a deadline, or give them one to make a decision, they will go right up to it without batting an eyelid, such is their inability to allow a crisis to dominate their behaviour.

The Mediterranean has an effect on all its peoples. Italians share with Spaniards a love of the haggle, only more so. They will haggle all day if you let them, especially over prices. On other matters they are, strangely, less concerned, be it delivery, quality or performance (though naturally they expect what they buy to work and generally what they sell does). Whereas Germans will pay more in order to get the proper quality or delivery, Italians will try to pay less in a time-honoured urge to save cash.

The country is divided along a north-south spectrum: the further south you are the less businesslike and commercial in a modern sense they will be, except when it comes to haggling over food and accommodation. The north is the most industrialized part of the country and the closest to European norms of business conduct.

There are plenty of business opportunities in Italy for selling or buying components or finished products and if the products are within their technology they will generally be of a high standard.

If they appear to be a little obsessed with their internal relationships and business contacts rather than with outsiders, this is because it is within those relationships that they find or seek their identity. Italy is like a large inward-looking society, only half-conscious of the world outside (like the Dutch, nobody else speaks their language), and, while they are open to outsiders, they do not adapt their customs and outlooks for them; outsiders remain observers not participants.

Italy remains very Italian – frantic, slightly inefficient, a trifle disorganized and in a hurry only to be late. It can be a rewarding place to do business in, providing you adjust to their culture and slow down to their tempo.

The Greeks

In Greece, a new member of the EEC (though its government has threatened to leave, which might just be their way of establishing a negotiating position), things are very Italian in tempo, only more so. The weather is hotter than in Italy and most business negotiations will take place in Athens or nearby, which is, or appears to be, even warmer (it's certainly dirtier and smoggier). So be properly dressed – a lightweight suit rather than casual.

Being less economically developed than the rest of the EEC, Greece still has a more traditional approach to business. Haggling at every level is expected (though please note: not by the police!) and even restaurants will accept a haggle over the bill. Food tends to turn up at the table lukewarm, even cold, and it takes a long time to consume it when in conversation with amiable people.

145

A lunchtime appointment can last all afternoon, assuming that it starts anywhere near the arranged time. If Italians are sometimes slack when it comes to punctuality, the Greeks appear never to have heard of the word, and they frequently cancel meetings unilaterally (how they ever managed to become a major maritime nation with their attitude to time I don't know).

In conversation you should avoid the subject of Turkey. I know it is a member of NATO along with Greece, but from my observation most Greeks appear to think they face a greater military danger from the Turks than they do from the Soviet Union. Whatever the reason for this feeling (and I once had it explained to me for several hours in a pavement restaurant in Athens by a former Cabinet minister, but the Domestica muddled my memory and I have forgotten what he said) it is best left alone as they feel quite strongly about it and might misinterpret your comments.

Apart from shipping, air travel and tourism, your business with Greece is likely to be in products of a less sophisticated range than with Germany. You will find them to be reliably honest in business matters but probably less than efficient in carrying out their commitments. The Mediterranean mañana mood prevails in most of their dealings but they have a traditional approach to money and know what is and what is not profitable.

Do not judge the wealth or success of the Greek negotiator by how he is dressed – what is comfortable for him may look rather untidy but he could very well be a millionaire or damn close to becoming one.

An American businessman I know who operates in the Middle East out of Athens told me that Greece is one place on the earth where the male chauvinist's adage is often true: you will seldom see a rich Greek with an unattractive woman. His advice, as a rule of thumb, is to work backwards from the relative good looks and figure of the woman that accompanies the untidy negotiator to an estimate of his wealth or position. The trouble with this advice is that most Greek women look (at least to me) like Aphrodite no matter who they are with.

The Spanish

At the other end of the Mediterranean we find the Spanish, an altogether different people from the Greeks. Spaniards are a proud, even haughty, people, much given to perceiving slights when none were intended, and always behaving, when they negotiate, as if they own the world, or the part of it that you are in.

Unlike the Greeks, they always dress for business and have a formal outlook on life and relationships (especially domestic arrangements) not found elsewhere in southern Europe.

To some extent it is incorrect to describe the people who live in Spain as Spaniards and in some parts you can cause great offence by doing so. The country is regionally divided, and, since Franco died, its regional dissimilarities have become more pronounced, particularly among the Basques and Catalonians who live in two of the most modern and industrialized regions.

Several regions have pronounced separatist political parties represented in either local assemblies or the Madrid parliament, and it is, therefore, wise not to stray into Spanish local politics if you intend to do business with them. (Nor is it wise to express opinions about bullfighting!)

The Spaniards lay great stress on personal honour and you will find that contracts entered into by them are strictly fulfilled and they expect no less from you. They have the Mediterranean knack for haggling and will do so without blushing, expecting you to do the same. But once agreed, the contract is not to be tampered with lightly. They would rather take a loss than admit openly that they have made a mistake – help them out (quietly) if you discover that they are suffering unintentionally from a deal and you will win a friend and ally for life.

A lot of business in Spain is either conducted or celebrated over the evening meal and you should be aware that they seldom sit down to eat their dinner before 9 p.m. – often it is closer to midnight. Hence, eat something earlier if you are likely to be hungry (and try if you can to avoid alcohol until you eat, otherwise you might well be careless when it counts).

The Portuguese, on the other hand, are a little more like the Greeks: informal, late for appointments, sociable and, except for the very rich, as poor, on the whole. They are also great friends of the British, Portugal being Britain's oldest ally.

The Dutch

The Dutch were at one time probably the most formal people in Europe and they are certainly still the tidiest (with the Swiss a wee skip behind). I don't know if Greece and the Netherlands do much business, but if they do it is a triumph of commercial spirit over cultural preference.

The Dutch older generation are ultra-clean and orderly and they like everything in business to be likewise. This probably explains some part of the deliberately untidy and almost unwashed revolt of the young against authority in the Netherlands – the young have simply turned their elders' behaviour upside down in an expression of (affluent) disapproval.

Because nobody else speaks their language the Dutch speak the languages of other lands and are very good linguists too. Almost everybody you will meet will speak English and/or German, so you should have no trouble negotiating, with more or less total understanding of your position on the part of your Dutch partners.

Traditionally, the Dutch have been very good with money and very conscious of its proper management, until, perhaps, recently when they have begun to spread around their tax income from North Sea gas with a very 'unDutch' casual abandon (though you should remember that the politics of this bonanza distribution are strictly the business of the Dutch people, who are not altogether anxious to receive your generous advice or criticism).

The Dutch are very good business negotiators, though they are a trifle ruthless when given their head. They think they can handle foreigners quite well and tend not to be nationalistic about the Netherlands (though they do not like to hear their country called 'Holland' which in fact refers to a couple of the provinces and not to the entire country). Being a small and vulnerable country they are the most 'European' of all the members of the EEC and can be impatient with 'little Englanders'.

Several of Europe's largest corporations have strong Dutch connections (Philips, Shell, Unilever etc.) and they are very good at building international business links. They are very competitive – for example, look at their ship salvage businesses – and they have a Germanic passion for getting the contract right, including exercising any economic leverage they can on you to secure additional advantages.

The Belgians

Across the border, the Belgians combine some of the characteristics of the Dutch with those of the French. To the north of Brussels the country is populated by the Flemish, a Dutch off-shoot from previous centuries, and to the south of the capital, there are the

French-speaking Belgians. Both communities have been locked into a highly complicated rivalry for many years, the details of which are not really your business and are best steered clear of.

The Belgians love to mix business with pleasure. They entertain a lot, and like to be entertained. This is one country where your expense account is going to be raided up to its limit. I once was negotiating in Bruges with a Belgian law firm about an indemnity my client had rashly signed, when my opposite number suggested we went to a little night club he knew. I agreed, being tired and thirsty. He didn't mention that the club was in a large mansion house near Maastrich in the Netherlands, a long drive away, and, once there, he clearly intended staying until breakfast time the next day. My feeble protests were over-ruled and we got back to my hotel in time for lunch, followed by a further round of negotiations that afternoon. So make sure you are fit and hearty before negotiating with Belgians, or better still avoid the social life until after the deal is settled.

The Scandinavians

As you go north in Europe you meet entirely different cultures. Collectively, the Norwegians, Danes, Swedes and Finns are known as Scandinavians and, on the surface, they have a great deal in common. When you get to know them you will begin to discern subtle differences.

On the whole Scandinavians are very civil, very polite and mostly formal in their relationships with foreigners. When they are together they tend to loosen up a bit, which is why their governments, if only to dampen their citizens' exuberance, have adopted extremely harsh drinking laws. (Never drink *anything* alcoholic and drive a car in Scandinavia; the police and local magistrates are never sympathetic and it will cost you enormous inconvenience to say the least.)

Sweden has an affluent population. Its wage costs are comparatively high and it can only survive economically by a deliberate policy of specialization. They are very serious about their business and invest heavily in modern technology to make sure that they are competitive around the world.

They will buy from you if you supply top-quality, excellent products that they need and which they cannot get locally; top quality is certainly what they will sell to you. They exist in world trade by the sheer excellence of their products and they seek high-value specialized segments of the markets that they export to rather than mass-volume low-margin sales in markets that their larger rivals triumph in.

Scandinavians do not go in for long price haggles and they expect that your proposition will be thoroughly worked out before it is presented to them. What changes they require will probably be minor, but on the whole if they are doing business with you at all it is because they have identified you as an expert firm in your market and they will expect your proposition to be as close to the best as is available. If they see glaring holes in your proposition they will revise their estimate of your professionalism and probably take their business elsewhere rather than argue with you over details which they think you ought to have got right the first time.

Swedes and Norwegians have a special problem in motivating their people to try harder to achieve more than they already are doing. I think this has something to do with the tax laws. Their governments have gone in for the redistribution of income in a big way (for the highest and purest of motives) and this tends to produce executives who reach for a level of achievement and then settle down to that level without pushing for more.

In other words, their entrepreneurial energies are confined to protecting what they have rather than expanding into where they could be; it is more common to find a Swedish or Norwegian firm fighting hard to cut costs in established product lines than it is to find them fighting for new business. They are not averse, however, to investing heavily in new technology (computers and satellites) if it helps them to stay ahead in their established markets (shipping for example).

On the import side they seek high-quality luxury consumer goods to meet the demands of their affluent citizens, but be warned: the high costs of distribution (especially wage and tax costs) compel them to squeeze hard on your price if they are to achieve the necessary mark-up on sales to ensure that they can pay their costs and make a small profit.

In Finland, where four large chains dominate the retail trade, you will have to compete very hard on price and quality to get your products into their shops, given extensive competition and a preference in the stores for buying local.

It is the affluence of the Scandinavian countries that is your opportunity: on the one hand it gives their citizens a lot to spend per head and on the other it forces them, through high domestic labour costs, to import high-volume, high-quality products that they find uneconomical to produce themselves.

The British

Turning to Britain and its negotiating styles we can discern certain basic characteristics common to all of its component parts. You should always remember (particularly if you are English) that the United Kingdom consists of four nations, not just one, and that they are moulded more or less firmly together.

The dominant nation is, of course, England. In fact much of the rest of the world refer to England (L'Angleterre, Englander etc.) when they really mean the United Kingdom. To be fair, most English people automatically speak of England as meaning Britain and in doing so when it is not appropriate they are unintentionally insensitive about the feelings of the Scots, Welsh and Irish.

The British share a common trait, which is that they have a wholly justified reputation for one business practice above all others: they have a lousy record for the late delivery of almost every product they produce. This is the single most consistent complaint of foreign importers of British goods and it is heard right across the surface of the planet.

Much has been written about this problem in the United Kingdom and much effort has been put in to do something about it. But it stubbornly refuses to be improved upon, and anyway is so entrenched in modern export folklore that even if it was improved upon it would still take years, if not generations, to eradicate it from the minds of customers all over the world.

Why does Britain have this deserved reputation? I do not know. In fact, I confess, I am part of it to an extent. The manuscript for this book was delivered fifteen months behind schedule to the publisher!

This always poses a problem when British managers are negotiating abroad. Having an identified weakness means that the negotiator is on the defensive and often has to accept terms for business that would otherwise be onerous. Importers can impose a delivery penalty on a British contract because it is credible for them to insist upon one. A British promise to deliver on time meets with the response that 'if you do deliver on time then you need not fear the penalty, but if you fear the penalty you are obviously unsure of your delivery'.

HOW NOT TO TACKLE A SUSPECTED RIP-OFF

I was minding my own business at Gothenberg airport when I was approached by a businessman who asked if I was travelling Club Class and if I was would I join him for a drink (I said 'yes' to both questions). He wanted to talk about something that was exciting him greatly and when he heard I was a consultant negotiator his tale poured forth.

Briefly, his story was that he had been selling children's clothes to a Swedish chain store for three years. On this visit he had arrived early and had taken time out to casually wander through one of the branches of this chain, and, naturally, he had gravitated to the children's department and looked out for his company's products.

What do you think he found? Yes! His clothes were there and were prominently displayed. This pleased him immensely and in his pride he informed the staff that he owned the firm that made what they were selling. They were most impressed and told him that there was a steady demand for his clothes, given their excellent quality.

He was in turn very pleased at this news and after a while he left. One thing, however, stuck in his mind and that was the price tag on one of his lines. It wasn't until he left that he realized that the Swedish Kroner price represented in sterling a mark-up of several hundred per cent on his selling price to the store.

When British companies had a world-wide lead in technology (the first economy to industrialize in the early nineteenth century) and a relative monopoly position in the old colonial Empire, they probably got into a habit of caring less about delivery than they ought to have done. After Hitler's war, from 1945 to about 1955, Britain once again had a substantial captive market with many of its rivals out of business until they repaired war damage. Again, the habit of being able to sell everything they could produce did little to wake them up to the essential requirements of a modern trading nation.

If delivery was the only criterion for trade then the United Kingdom could suffer a catastrophic collapse in its exports until it did something about its failings. Fortunately, delivery is only one of

Such was his concern that he went back to the shop and noted down all the prices of every one of his products. He worked out the mark-up and found it was consistent throughout – the chain store, which had always pleaded poverty and tight competition as reasons for squeezing his prices, was, he said, 'ripping me off'.

He was upset about this, even though the price he had got for his products was profitable to his business. He raised this immediately with them in the negotiations later that morning and told them he felt they had been cheating him. They were obviously offended at this charge but after much discussion they agreed to raise their purchase prices. They claimed this would squeeze their profits because of their very high labour costs and taxes on their stores.

He was now even more worried because he felt he had over-reacted and gone in too strong and perhaps damaged his good relationships. I suggested it would have been better if he had raised the question of their retail pricing policy quite neutrally and let the implications of that lead them to either a credible defence of their mark-up or to a revision of their purchase price. By charging in he had risked causing offence when none was necessary and whatever he had gained in the immediate trip might be followed by a falling off in orders as they eased out an obviously disgruntled supplier. By paying him more they partly confirmed his feeling of being cheated, whether this was the case or not.

several aspects of British produce and in many cases it is not the all-important one.

Britain is a major trading nation; though its share of the growing volume of world trade is falling, it is still expanding its absolute output of exports. One reason among others for this credible performance is the technical competence of its industries and the sheer inventiveness of its scientific and engineering people. This strengthens the hand of negotiators plying their products across the world.

Technology is not monopolized by the British and there is a warning here in the so-called 'sunrise' industries (communications, for example); Britain may not have the technical capacity to keep its share of world trade from declining very rapidly once new technologies pass to rivals.

Until that unhappy (for the British) outcome, negotiations are by no means a one-way street for the British. Being clobbered with 'low delivery morale' (in other words, Britain's trading partners do not believe what they are promised) and countering with technological excellence is a regular scene in negotiations between Britain and the rest of the world. As long as British negotiators can keep the balance between their company's strengths and weaknesses in their favour they will be around the international trading scene for long enough.

It is only recently that the majority of export-oriented business negotiators have developed a consistent policy of face-to-face contact with their clients in foreign climes. There is no doubt that British companies have been poor at regular service visits compared with their rivals. Partly, it is in response to the very good records of their rivals in this respect that British firms have reacted so positively. And there is no doubt that, if you want to maintain high sales volume in export markets, regular high-level visits are essential. Not only does it do you good with a client, it also does you good indirectly by bolstering the status and morale of the local agents.

This leads to another weakness of the British negotiator, namely the lack of a proclivity for languages other than native English. There is a minor arrogance about speakers of English as a mother tongue; they assume that everybody else in the world knows, or wants to know, how to speak English. Again, it reflects the old Empire (and the one before that in the Americas) and is not going to change quickly (nor is Britain encouraged to do so by the behaviour of the rest of the world which learns English as a second language – with the exception, of course, of the French who especially insist on speaking French with English speaking visitors).

The EEC might change Britain's mono-dependence on one language, particularly as Britain's trade with the EEC now accounts for over 40 per cent of its total trade. But, for the most part, negotiations with British firms will take place in English, literature will be printed in English and for many firms little compromise will be visible in the matter of things foreign.

Of the nations that make up Britain, the English, being the largest in population (46 million out of 54 million), are the ones that set the pace in international business. The English have a reputation for being gentlemen (generally very honest in their dealings even when things go against them), though for the most part they are

STYLES OF NEGOTIATING

European, American, and Japanese

European	American	Japanese
State capitalist	Competitive capitalist	Welfare capitalist
Traditional individualism	Self-reliant individualism	Traditional collectivism
Status by background	Status by success	Status by position
Personal leadership	Personal leadership	Group consensus
Integrity oriented	Reward oriented	Respect oriented
Impatient	Very impatient	Patient
Fairly formal	Informal	Formal
Short preliminaries	Few preliminaries	Long preliminaries
Fair offers	Reasonable offers	Sky-high offers
Modest concessions	Little concessions	Large concessions
Item by item trade	Item by item trade	Linked package deal
Considerable authority	Total authority	No authority
Persuasive tactics	Aggressive tactics	Consensus tactics
Logical arguments	Arguments	Needs analysis
Promises	Threats	Commitments
'Good deal'	'Best deal'	'Long-term deal'
Not losing	Winning	Succeeding

merely amateurs. More than 80 per cent of British managers, for instance, are totally unqualified – only 7 per cent have university degrees! Their approach to business is well short of professional standards and they compare badly with overseas executives.

This means that they appear at negotiations poorly prepared, can be inflexible in the critical phases (re-packaging and bargaining), and do not exert much energy. It is no accident that most of the high-profile successful entrepreneurs in the UK are not native born (Robert Maxwell, Tiny Roland, Charles Forte, Rupert Murdoch and Nazmu Virani to name a few), and the lack of, or rather decline in, flair is nowhere better demonstrated than in the successful emergence of the post-war immigrant shopkeepers and small businessmen as displacers of indigenous owners.

Amateurism in business management is seen in the stubbornness of British negotiators – an almost take-it-or-leave-it attitude. No wonder so many traditional businesses have succumbed to take-overs and re-organization from entrepreneurs who have understood the changing markets of Europe and are ready to try something out that is new. Poor investment, indifferent quality, poor delivery and unreliability are not features that give grounds for pride.

If a British firm can get these factors right, it can do wonders in the world. The fact that so many deals are concluded by British negotiators that do make a profit and do win repeat business suggests that the British are not entirely hopeless. It is, however, a national characteristic to be self-effacing when we are not self-denigrating.

As for the Scots, they divide into two types: those that live and work in Scotland and those that live and work in other parts of the world. Of the first group, we can assume that they are fairly well resourced in a financial sense, though this tends to make them very cautious, sometimes beyond the point where enterprise can flourish. The second group, often rise high in their adopted communities while keeping their financial sense about them.

Given the relatively few opportunities to run a really large business in Scotland (its economic base is one-tenth that of the UK and much of its key industry is run from elsewhere in the world; only the financial centre of Edinburgh is an exception to this rule and much of that sends its funds elsewhere), many of the most talented negotiators go south to England, or even further afield, and they combine a hard-headed nose for business with the scope given them by their new environment. It can lead to very successful business careers.

A Scot will always concentrate on the financial aspects of a deal ('we're in it for the money not the glory!') but having little to trade they are in the smaller league internationally.

The European tribes

Doing business with the European tribes ought to be equivalent to doing business with the trillion-dollar economy of the United States, except that the barriers to business within Europe, including within the EEC countries, mean that there is nothing like the freedom of doing business between the states of the US of A. The customs union of the EEC now has bigger and more intrusive customs procedures than it had when the countries were entirely separate. Harmonization of business practice across the EEC countries is a long way from being achieved, as it has been in the United States.

This leads business negotiators to require not just the skills of trading and bargaining but also requires of them that they immerse themselves in the cultural and business norms of their neighbours.

Given that learning a country's language is conducive to learning how to negotiate with the people that speak it, those continental negotiators who have a facility for learning their neighbours' languages are much better placed to do business in Europe than the British who tend to be ignorant of any language but their own.

How long this will continue in the light of the increasing intra-European trade of even the British remains to be seen, but for the moment the other Europeans have an advantage.

That the old barriers between the tribes of Europe might break down is still only a possibility for the more distant future, but two things are for sure: firstly, if harmonization does occur it will still be shaded by the individualism of the originating countries (you will still know the difference between doing business in Greece and Norway, for example); and, secondly, it won't happen in a hurry.

1 (a) Very good! German companies often try this one on, knowing that they are good payers and that foreigners like to do business with them (many companies believe that a German clientele is a good advertisement for them to have). If you can't say no try *(c)*. (10)

   (b) You are the kind of negotiator that the Germans like to do business with – it makes up for those others who know what their products are worth. If the Germans could get your steels at home they would not bother dealing with you and, if you are British, risking late deliveries. (-10)

   (c) At least you are trying to limit the damage. It is always best to make a conditional proposition, even if you are surrendering! (5)

2 (a) A risky policy as it may cause a breakdown in your longer-term relationship. They may have a good reason for a pricing policy that involves an 800 per cent mark-up. If they raise their purchase price from you this will confirm that they are ripping you off, if they don't you will still be unhappy. (-10)

   (b) A safe policy, though it leaves you without information as to your case for a price increase. (5)

   (c) Probably a sensible *first* move to be followed by *(b)*. As you have raised this issue without prompting they may wonder why you have done so and if they are cheating you their embarrassment might show. At the next price negotiation they have the face option of moving up your prices. (10)

   (d) The rational move, but in business nobody likes to take out less than they can and if you follow this policy either you are ripping them off silly or you have saintly tendencies! (7)

3 (a) Only if the pound sterling is riding high. (-5)

   (b) Not really. The British government has a habit of throwing money at potential customers – it has been known to borrow money from the Swiss at 14 per cent and lend it to the Poles at 7 per cent to pay for supplying the Poles with heavily subsidized ships. If the communists can get deals like that, what do you rate your chances as being? (-15) *(c)* Absolutely right. The worst problem of British exports is simply delivery, on time and when agreed. If you don't impose penalty payments on the British for poor delivery – which will almost certainly have to be paid to you and which will therefore reduce the actual cost of the products – you are simply not trying. (10)

(d) Not really. British products are generally of high quality and of advanced technology. This is often sufficient compensation for poor delivery. (-10)

Self-assessment test 10

1 You are stopped by a policeman in Ogoland and he demands that you pay him 50 quonks (about £2) not to book you for speeding. You were almost stationary at the time and could not have been speeding at all. Do you tell him:

  (a) Not before you see your consul?

  (b) You do not pay bribes?

  (c) Certainly, if he has change for a 100 quonk note?

2 A Nigerian importer of household paraffin-driven electricity generators with whom you have dealt successfully in the past places an order worth £230,000 and requires deliveries to commence in three months. He agrees to pay against invoices on despatch and requires an unconditional performance bond from you for 10 per cent of the value of the order. Do you:

  (a) Agree providing he opens a confirmed, irrevocable letter of credit through your own bank for the £230,000 payable on despatch of the first batch of generators?

  (b) Decline to sign an unconditional performance bond that is payable on demand?

  (c) Agree because you desperately need his business to avoid major redundancies in your plant?

3 An Indian importer owes you £100,000 and you demand payment before any more shipments take place. He tells you he is going through a short-term cash flow crisis and needs more time to pay and that he cannot pay if he does not get more of your products. Do you:

  (a) Tell him he cannot get more deliveries unless he pays what he owes?

  (b) Tell him that if he does not pay you will sue him?

  (c) Decide to visit him in India and see for yourself what his financial situation is really like?

  (d) Tell him if he pays you £20,000 on account you will make another delivery?

11 Pure as the driven mud

*or, how it is when you trade
in the Third World*

The bad news

First, we should dispose of the bad news. The Third World (roughly everywhere other than where we have already been in previous chapters) is a long way from being a happy and prosperous place in which to do business. Apart from having some of the worst poverty on the planet (though they are not by any means *all*, nor even the majority, starving), some of the worst records in health and hygiene, much of the worst records in education and welfare, and a long history of neglect and failure, the countries that comprise the Third World also have an unenviable record for both local violence and general warfare.

Since 1945, the majority of wars (119 out of 124) have taken place in the Third World, while most systems of government are of military origin, and many of the governments that have come to power there have done so not by means of an election but from military coups or by violent civil wars and revolution.

Hence, low levels of personal income, political instability, and local violence are features of the Third World that have to be borne in mind by the international business negotiator when contemplating business in these countries. Legal foundations for conducting business have been laid in most of these countries, and for many of them there is more than a semblance of law and order. But the fact remains that there are wide variations in standards and conduct in many of these countries and it is not always possible to seek, let alone get, redress for breaches of contract – in fact, in some places even to seek redress is to invite judicial and extra-judicial reprisals against one's business and, sometimes, one's person.

The scale of corruption

Standards of public service in respect of personal ethics and morality are not always of the kind that is expected by a person living in a relatively uncorrupt Western democracy. It is always dangerous to generalize about moral issues – 'let he who is without guilt first cast a stone' etc. – and you are not advised to do so except in an abstract fashion (and always while safely in your own backyard). But corruption, the great unspoken feature of business in the Third World, is a reality of business which few are prepared for when they are confronted with its scale and, what appears to be worse, its total acceptance as a way of life.

In corrupt societies (that is, those judged to be corrupt by normal Western standards; though be careful of being too pompous about this in case tomorrow's papers expose some local scandals in your own country) the norm is for almost everybody who has some discretionary power, no matter how trivial, to use that discretion to personal advantage in return for some small, and not so small, consideration.

Passports get stamped faster if a small token payment (called 'dash' in West Africa) is left within the pages when it is handed over – otherwise, you might be left to the end of the queue even if you were first to get to the counter. Similarly, in customs, immigration and the baggage reclaim area.

Success in securing airline reservations tends to be correlated with a small bribe to the booking clerk; seat reservations likewise. Anything that needs rubber stamping is a goldmine to the clerk who has the rubber stamp. If he has to consult another clerk's list or check with a supervisor, you had better bear this in mind when handing over the bribe because what is divided by two or three is often not enough to generate an interest in your interests in those with no incentive to take an interest in your interests!

Hotel reservations can appear at the drop of a 100 cedi note, and disappear if somebody got there before you with a 200 cedi note. The lift shaft vista awaits those foolish enough to trust to their confirmed reservation with the ocean view, if they forget to 'dash' the desk clerk. A table by the toilets in the restaurant is your best chance if you forget to look after the head waiter, and you might as well be *in* the toilet if you forget to demonstrate to the waiters serving the tables your goodwill and intention to see them all right – the best way to ensure the latter is to tip them when they take the order and imply that there is more to follow.

As for official forms, you have little hope of even getting near one in many countries without paying the clerk the local 'tax' on those forms which are a devolved responsibility of the clerk who collects the forms. Pay up and you get the form; don't and you will wait, perhaps for ever.

Risks of mishandling the pay-off

Once petty corruption becomes a way of life and spreads right across the entire fabric of society, it is something you have to accept as a visitor if you wish to do any business at all. You should take local guidance on the state of play regarding corruption and follow the advice of the 'old hands'.

It is not only an expensive business but also a risky one. If you assume everybody is corrupt and they are not you might get into serious trouble for attempting to bribe an honest clerk, or worse for you, an honest policeman. Several businessmen at any one time are in local jails for trying to corrupt officialdom. Perhaps the (corrupt) authorities are trying to make an example of them for PR purposes, or perhaps the businessmen did not offer a big enough bribe in the negotiations and they are in jail for the 'insult'.

A stranger in a Third World country has no means of knowing whether the police (or army) have stopped him or her for a real offence or because they want to collect some extra pocket money.

Two basic rules should be applied in these circumstances. First, and without exception, you should never stand on your dignity and imply either by word, grimace or gesture that the official who has stopped you does not have authority to do so, or that he is in any way unsuited to be in the position he is in, or that he is in some sense incompetent, a candidate for the gestapo, or 'typical' of his race, religion or nation.

Secondly, you must not make a direct approach to the subject of bribery (unless, as can happen, they tell you straight out that they want some pay-off for letting you go, in which case, pay up and go).

Your best bet, when not sure of the scene, is to apologize for whatever wrong they claim that you have committed (even if you feel indignant because of your saint-like innocence) and say words to the effect: 'I am a stranger in your country, officer, Sir, and I am very sorry for my mistake, Sir. In my country we pay on the spot fines for similar offences and if you tell me, Sir, what the fine is I will pay it to you immediately, Sir.'

Either (unlikely) he will tell you that you do not pay fines on the spot in Ogoland but will have to appear in court next Monday and pay any fine then, or (more likely) he will tell you what you have to pay him. As long as you say the above with no money in sight (don't reach into your pocket for your wallet until told to do so), you are unlikely to be charged with attempting to bribe an officer of the law. If he asks you for money and you pay him you are unlikely to have further trouble.

So keep your smart comments to yourself, pay up and get going.

If you cannot bring yourself to do this, well and good. But in that case be ready for a long hassle, an uncomfortable time in detention and perhaps, in some countries, a few indignities and bruises to your person. While the latter is going on you may wish to review your decision to be an international negotiator in the Third World.

Rackets in quotas, permissions, and licences

In India, up to recently, public corruption was so widespread that it was a safe bet that you could offer a bribe – even for a rail ticket – and expect to get appropriate treatment. Many members of India's many governments are widely suspected of being involved in big pay-offs from this or that interest to smooth the way over the many obstacles to the conduct of business that have been created by India's central government.

Believing, as it does, that intervention is necessary if India is to be developed industrially and commercially, the government in New Delhi has introduced thousands of regulations and licences for all forms of trade, including exports and imports, and these have become 'dripping roasts' for the officials who have discretion on how the regulations are applied and to whom the licences are doled out.

Whenever a government is persuaded by somebody to have a quota for this or that (in the 'national interest') they create a meal ticket for the clerk who has control of the quotas. In Nigeria and Ghana businesses have grown up in the trade of licences and quotas – not of the goods that are meant to be licensed or quotad!

An official quota to import shoes is traded across the business community for fabulous sums long before a single pair of shoes reaches the country. I know one businessman in Ghana who bought the production licence for shirts and is sitting on it until somebody else comes along to buy it at a price considerably more profitable to him than actually laying out the capital to make shirts.

When somebody does come along who wants to manufacture shirts he will still have to get another permission to erect the buildings and that permission too can provide a good living for the person who gets hold of it first, without them ever having to go through the trauma of actually building and operating a manufacturing plant.

Negotiating in these conditions to set up an import distribution network for your shoes, or a plant to manufacture them locally, is not going to be a simple process of putting up a proposition to somebody and letting them evaluate the commercial prospects. You will have no idea how serious the opposite number is about actually doing anything about your proposition. He may only be interested in tying you into a deal to secure the appropriate paper licence for somebody (anybody) to implement your proposition so that he can re-sell the licence to a third party.

If the project is complex and on a large scale, the number of officials that have to be 'squared' can reach formidable numbers. The costs of 'seeing them all right' will not be trivial, and for that reason they are not likely to be accountable (that is, you have no assurance of the efficiency of your bribes nor whether the people whom you thought or were persuaded to believe needed to be squared received anything at all). You could be the victim of a con as well as a candidate to become a convict (and in much of Africa there are more conmen out of jail than in it).

The market in official permissions is only one side of the deal; in many areas where central control is not as strong and certain as it should be (and sometimes even under the very noses of official personnel) you might be subject to an unofficial market in permissions.

You will have to pay off the local 'bosses' (or those who convince you that they are local bosses) or suffer the risk of severe retribution to your person and property (if your trucks are burnt out you know they were not kidding you). Lawlessness of this kind is a natural by-product of the system of official corruption. For the unofficial 'tax' collectors who do not have an official goldmine of discretion at their disposal, their remedy is to invent one, and where necessary to back it up with threats, intimidation and outright violence.

If this seems incredible, you should consider the well-known operations of the Mafiosa in parts of southern Italy and the pay-offs they require, in addition to whatever permissions you have obtained from the authorities. You might also consider the very large-scale operations of the 'Godfathers' of Northern Ireland who 'tax' all kinds of businesses, allegedly to replenish their paramilitary funds but more often to support their personal life styles – and this

HEALTH, TRAVEL AND HAPPINESS

I know several British expatriates who have made lucrative livings from acting as middle-men between 'associates' of the Kenyan government and major overseas investors in Kenya. Some of them found they could not get their wealth out of Kenya when they came to retire and they face the rest of their lives in lonely but affluent splendour in Nairobi or Mombassa (with the real attendant risk that they may be exposed and expelled as the old elite moves over), when in fact they would rather return relatively rich and more or less safe to whence they hail from, usually somewhere in the south of England.

In the interests of international understanding, I agreed to help one of these gentlemen develop a scheme to get as much of his money out of Kenya as was possible, without his risking losing the lot if he was caught trying to do so. I also insisted that my scheme would not be illegal.

My scheme involved the use of the so-called 'medical expenses' dodge and a side-line deal in unused airline tickets. My fee for this service was to be 5 per cent of the gross amount he got out of Kenya plus expenses.

First he needed a local doctor to prescribe him as a heart patient (easily achieved on the 'old hands' circuit) who needed urgent medical attention in Harley Street, London.

Then I had to find someone in the UK who would agree to 'treat' him for his complaint. The catch was that he was to 'need' treatment regularly – every three months in London – and the doctor was to charge a large fee each time for doing so. On each trip he was also allowed to take some personal income for expenses.

with the armed authorities patrolling the same streets looking for them!

Large-scale projects are likely to be negotiated at the highest levels. Nobody ever did much in the way of large-scale projects in Kenya who did not pass before the Presidential desk when Jomo Kenyatta (and Mrs Kenyatta!) ran the show. Similarly in President Sadat's Egypt, though the front man there was his brother, while in the Philippines everything has been run for many years through President and Mrs Marcos.

The difference between the fee actually paid to the doctor and the invoice charged on my client's bank in Nairobi was to be paid into my client's bank account in the UK.

The second part of the plan involved my client purchasing in Kenya first-class round-the-world tickets each time he and his wife had to fly to London for his 'medical' attention. He would use these tickets to get to London and I placed the unused portion of the ticket with a pal in the travel business at a discounted price.

The unused portion was sold on to a manager of an international export business who used the discounted (first-class) tickets to fly on to various parts of the world. Airlines will not refund cash for airtickets sold in Third World countries but did, at that time, allow various changes of destination and dates of travel in the tickets as long as the overall price was not altered (recently even this dodge was stopped if the tickets were issued in certain countries) and they never take any notice of the name on the ticket.

After a year using this plan my pal managed to extract over £92,000 net into the UK. Naturally I wanted my 5 per cent of the gross amount plus my expenses.

So if any reader knows the whereabouts of a certain 'gentleman' recently resident in Kenya who is in excellent health and has a pocket full of first-class round-the-world tickets for sale, I would appreciate it greatly if you would pass his present address to me – he owes me about £6,000!

(Moral: if you arrange cash deals, get paid cash, preferably in advance (on the hooker's principle) and always as you go along, especially when dealing with 'pals'.)

In Nicaragua the Somoza family ran the entire country as if it was a private bank account and they went to such excesses that most of the population preferred to take their chances with the communists rather than continue to live under the family's rule. This shows how desperate they must have been, for communists in power are every bit as despotic as those they throw out – only worse, no communist government has ever demitted office once it has established itself.

If you are dealing with the top you are sure of at least one thing: if you get the go-ahead the project is likely to become a reality eventually (though if they tap your brain and discover that they can do the job themselves and cream off the profits, you might find yourself the creator of a good idea and *persona non grata* on an early flight home!).

You will need presidential level approval to get the otherwise lethargic system to move in your favour. But presidents and their families cannot supervise everything and you will have to rely on people a little lower in the structure to get things moving. This might cost you (I avoid any reference at all to what 'presidential approval' could cost you in some countries and, in the interests of not having a future visa blocked, certainly cast no aspersions on the countries mentioned above!).

First World corruption too

Before you feel a little smug about all this frank talk of corruption in Third World countries, you should pause a little and look around the First World. There are scams everywhere. The only difference is that most of them are unusual and in Western democracies those who indulge in them are chased and prosecuted if caught.

By way of illustration, I read of a restaurant in Hollywood where the rich, famous and glamorous (and those who wanted to be thought as such) dined *if* they could get a table. The head waiter ran a very lucrative side business for a year or more before vexed and frustrated clients complained to the owner about his rip-offs.

The owner had no idea of the scam as he was too busy creating the wonderful food in the kitchen to know what his people out front were up to. To get a table in this 'in-scene', diners had to slip $100 bills to the waiter before he would take them to a table (and it being Hollywood where stars are a dime a dozen he was not in any way star-struck even when really 'big' names came in looking for a burger and chips). He must have grossed tens of thousands of dollars before being 'shopped' to the owner.

So all those who have tipped a waiter for giving them a 'nice' table (and there are always nicer tables than the one you have been shunted to) must accept that this petty fiddle is widespread throughout 'civilization'.

Politicians are often in the news for one of their esteemed number being forced to resign on clouds of corruption charges. Britain ran into a whole series of these unfortunate incidents in the 1970s, and a US Vice President resigned accused of accepting favours from constituents.

CASH OR KIND

Exchange regulations and controls can be extremely tight in certain countries because the government desires to use the country's foreign currency earnings with the greatest care and attention to political priorities. The penalties for breaches of these regulations can be severe – imprisonment for offenders, confiscation of property (and not just the bag full of dollars you were caught with) and heavy fines are among them.

Many have been tempted to engage in illegal dodges to get round the problem.

For example, in some countries you can arrange to have payment made to you not in the form of cash but in real goods which you then sell-on to recover your money. If you are unable to get paid in dollars in Ghana but can acquire good quality cocoa against payment in local cedis you can ship out the cocoa to Europe and sell it for hard currency. The fact that you have to pay CIF may mean you taking a loss on the original amount owed to you – but in a choice between a loss and a total loss you don't really have a choice!

To obviate the cost of shipping real goods out you can try some high-value item which you can take with you, though here you run the risk of being stopped at customs and searched. Diamonds, gold, artifacts and such-like are too obvious for even the dimmest customs official to miss (and by no means assume that customs officials in other countries are any less smart than they are in your own).

I know a negotiator who has avoided currency regulations for years by the simple expedient of using local currency to buy rare stamps which he sticks in his wallet and sells in London. Two things favour his choice of payment: he knows a rare stamp when he sees one and, though he has been searched at customs several times, nobody has yet noticed his postage stamps!

A famous US rip-off concerned the owner of a soya oil storage depot in the United States. The soya oil, for which there was a government subsidy, was stored in a series of interlinked tanks. When government inspectors checked the tanks they always found them full and the owner received the subsidy. Unbeknown to the inspectors, the owner was able to show a full tank by pumping oil from a master tank to each subsidiary one. In fact, he was being paid a subsidy for several million gallons while having only a few thousand in stock. Unfortunately, one day his pumps broke down during an inspection!

A similar fiddle went on for years in the UK in respect of subsidies to hill farmers. Each sheep was subsidized by the Ministry of Agriculture which sent inspectors round to check the numbers. The farmers simply moved the same sheep from hill to hill while driving the inspector the long way round the farm. He counted the same sheep over and over, and the the farmer got the subsidy.

The fact remains, however, that even with the incidental examples of corruption in the West, corruption is nothing like on the scale that you will find in the Third World at all levels of their societies. If this raises for you deeply felt moral issues, you will have to overcome them some way or do your business elsewhere.

Legislators pass laws against corruptly seeking business abroad, and moral leaders often make speeches condemning it, but the combined effect of laws and condemnation has not been sufficient to stem the practice.

Go-betweens

Open or thinly disguised corruption – paying off go-betweens for securing multi-million dollar business – has proven to be vulnerable to inquiry and, if established, to prosecution in the home country of the business concerned (even if ignored in the country where the pay-off for the order occurred). Hence, big-business negotiators have become more subtle about disguising the bribes – known euphemistically as 'commissions' – and they have become more careful to cover their tracks.

To use a go-between in itself indicates that you expect a commission will have to be paid, for no go-between (yet) has got business for an overseas company for nothing.

Some large corporations contribute to party funds in the country they do business in and, in return, they are allowed special concessions to do their business.

In Zimbabwe, for example, several major trading corporations have strong links with the government, and some have links with all the major political figures in the country. This is not necessarily a case of financial corruption; the firms concerned arrange mutually beneficial contacts for the Zimbabwe government abroad, do favours for government personnel in their official capacities, and make special donations to official activities without any implication that the individuals in government personally benefit from this relationship.

In sum, you will have to decide how you are going to cope with this problem. At the lowest level of getting into and around a country you will have to tip, bribe, dash, baksheesh, or commission those whose co-operation is necessary for you to function there. Once you cross that line (and be sure that you will have to do so) you will be faced with another line (and yet another!) as the sums at stake become progressively larger.

You can leave it to a go-between and let him deal with the officials that 'need taking care of', or you can take care of them yourself. But be clear: there is no legal way to bribe somebody and you are personally vulnerable once you attempt to do so.

Paying them in their own country out of the money for the deal is one way to settle up (which leaves you exposed when you hand over the cash), while paying them through bank accounts abroad (the famous numbered Swiss account system) is as risky.

To set up a money deal with a Swiss bank on behalf of somebody else will involve your own staff and you are then vulnerable to their mood and sense of grievance in future if something goes wrong with your relationship with them (many 'office romances' that go sour end up with the boss in court on charges varying from income tax evasion to bribery – 'hell hath no fury' etc. – so protect yourself from the same by *never* chasing your own staff).

Your go-between may swear undying loyalty and confidentiality to you and your company in accepting the bribe but, given the human rights records of many of these countries, you cannot be sure that he will remain so adamant in defence of your interests once handed over to the tender mercies of interrogators who do not recognize the Geneva Convention when they question prisoners, and have orders to find out who gave them the money, how much was given and where the money is now.

Your next, innocent, visit to that country could be the prelude to some very uncomfortable experiences (if you think Third World hotels have a long way to go before they are comfortable, you should compare them with their prisons!).

The bribery of tips

I have never heard anybody give satisfactory advice on how to cope with this problem in business, and not just in the Third World. There is a thin, almost transparent line between a gift for goodwill and a gift as an inducement.

At Christmas, in Europe, firms send out sometimes lavish gifts to their clients. A case of whisky is lavish in anybody's terms and when it lands on the desk of a named individual who happens to be the buyer of your products, can you be sure that this is no more than a seasonal gesture of goodwill etc.? (Some companies, in an effort to prevent inducement of key personnel, insist that all gifts from suppliers and clients are pooled and shared out among the entire staff – to get round this, some suppliers send their Christmas gifts to the home address of the staff they wish to 'cultivate'.)

And what of taking potential clients to lunch? I have lost count of the lunches I have given or been given over the years, though I have never lost any sleep over the ethics involved (I have lost sleep on occasion from the food and drink partaken at these events!).

The giving and receiving of gifts is a delicate area in business and only the circumstances and intentions of those involved can really decide on which side of the thin line gift-swapping falls.

When we receive exceptional service we often reward it in some way – a tip, a letter of commendation, a profuse thank you etc. – and in some places it pays to tip the service before you receive it in order to make sure that you enjoy it.

To arrive empty-handed at a private home for dinner with a business associate can appear to be less than polite. Hence, many people go to some lengths to ensure that they arrive with some flowers, chocolates, perfume, or brandy etc. for the lady or gentleman of the house. Others follow up an evening's socializing with a business partner with a small gift for the children.

In some countries there is an expectation that those whom you deal with receive some gift, the nature and expense of the gift varying from one country to another. In the Philippines, gifts reflecting personal gratitude for favours received are on a scale unlikely to be accepted in other countries. Business partners, and those who would wish to become so, can engage in gift-swapping in the price range of $1000 plus without embarrassing each other; in Spain, gifts in the biro pen range are more likely to be acceptable.

NAÏVETÉ IS NO DEFENCE

Many years ago when I had just started as a salesman I chanced upon what I thought was a great opportunity to make a large and relatively certain sale and, in my enthusiasm, I did not take enough care to think through its legalities.

I had been discussing with a buyer the products I was selling – industrial spraying equipment – and after my sales pitch the conversation went on to non-business matters. The buyer – a young man of my own age – had just passed his driving test and was very keen to buy his first car. His problem: he did not have the necessary deposit.

I went away, but thought over the selling sequence and his conversation about his desire for a car came back to mind. I was on a company car purchase scheme – the monthly payments were made by my company out of my sales commission and I wondered if we could offer the buyer something similar.

I asked my boss if he had any objection as to who got the discount we were able to offer on our products and accessories. He said 'no' as long as we got the order.

I then explained what I intended to offer the young buyer. We would supply his company's spraying needs but at full list price. In return for the initial order we would put up the deposit on a new car for him. If he ensured that we received a regular monthly order for spares, paint and hoses we would continue to pay the monthly payments on his car out of the discount we would normally have given his company for purchasing our products.

My boss said 'go ahead'. The buyer went for the deal immediately and was driving a new mini within a week of our receiving his first order.

Sometime later I was in conversation with other sales staff at a 'Thank God It's Friday' seminar and re-told the story, much to the horror of the senior salesmen. They quickly informed me that the entire proposition was illegal as it was tantamount to offering an inducement, that is, bribery. I was appalled at my stupidity. Naturally, I never did such a disreputable thing again!

Commercial risks can be insured against and the extent of international trade ensures that insurance is a huge industry. Premiums are fixed for all kinds of transaction in all parts of the world and where losses occur the losers can collect their insurance. At least in theory. More than one claimant has been surprised by the small print that cuts their claims well below their losses. The time to negotiate the small print is before you sign it. Insurers will make special agreements with you provided that you do so before they accept your risks. Otherwise you will be offered their standard terms.

The insurance companies employ 'loss adjusters' who travel the globe to assess the extent of the losses by claimants and, where appropriate, to negotiate a settlement, sometimes with third parties. A friend of mine is a loss adjuster for a London syndicate and he spends most of his time visiting West Africa, particularly Nigeria. He claims to be able to spot a fraudulent claim at half a mile and always delights in finding a way to reduce the net cost of a payout by an ingenious application of the principles of salvage to property. In one case he arranged for an (arson) burnt-out factory to be cleared inside where the roof had collapsed and turned into a 'walled lorry park'. This reduced a total loss to a partial loss.

Insurance companies pay out when they receive legitimate claims and they are prepared to pursue remedies through the courts when this is necessary, where they suspect fraud or other illegal acts. Much could be written about negotiating with insurance companies over claims. The most that can be said about the prospects of bettering insurance companies in negotiation can be summed up in the observation that insurance executives, like bookies, seldom go bust and most of them are fairly well off.

If they get their premium levels right, then the cost of paying out on claims is more than covered by what they take in from people who are of a pessimistic disposition (bearing in mind that the insurance company in quoting a premium is judging that the insured risk will not occur and the person seeking the insurance is saying that it will).

To assist in promoting exports, the governments of most European countries have established funds to supplement insurance coverage for those risks that a commercial insurance partnership will not cover. In Britain, the Export Credit Guarantee

Department (ECGD) will quote an exporter against the risk of default on payment caused by, say, a collapse of a country's credit system through war, revolution and general mayhem. The charge for this is related to their estimates of the risk. Faced with the prospect of a total loss the British exporter can pay a premium and get covered for most of the cost of his exports (which also helps sometimes to raise credit for the company). Germany, France, Spain and Italy run similar schemes.

Errors of judgement, however, are still made. Firms can still take risks (thus saving on premium costs) or they may find themselves not to be sufficiently covered to recompense them fully if a possible situation becomes a reality. When the timing of insurance coverage and its acceptance by those concerned is out of phase with commercial pressures to sign and be damned, there is always the real possibility that something will happen (Murphy's Law) before the paperwork is completed. At this point the exporter is on his own and the losses could be crippling.

On getting paid

The next largest problem after that of the morality of paying 'commissions' to smooth the path of doing profitable business is the simple, and ultimately more important one, of getting paid for your products. Securing business is only one aspect of staying in business. You have to get paid for what you deliver and this can be a problem when dealing with clients a long way from the reach of your own courts (it is sometimes difficult to get paid even when clients are just across the road from your own local County Court).

International trade would be inhibited greatly if some means had not been found to ensure that suppliers got paid by importers. There is much that can go wrong between an order being signed and the cash for the product arriving safely in your bank account.

In a society where commercial contracts are protected by the full force of the law there is always the remedy of suing somebody who has not paid for your products. This works more or less efficiently but it is, or can be, very expensive to get justice. Winning a legal case may still leave you with losses if you cannot collect on the compensation.

Where the law is weak – or heavily biased in favour of local people (a not uncommon feature in parts of the world – his uncle may not only be his partner, he may also be the local magistrate!) – recourse to lawyers may not be your best solution to a payments problem. Calling in the lawyers could set you back in your quest to be paid if the local businessman regards such action as an affront to his 'integrity'.

Hence, whereas a detailed grasp of the intricacies of the law of international contract is a necessary attribute for the international negotiator, it certainly is not sufficient by itself. A good deal more is needed, much of it common sense and some of it the result of hard earned experience.

One of the most common ways of paying for goods is for the buyer to open a letter of credit in favour of the seller. Negotiators have to watch the conditions that are attached to such a letter – these are negotiable and as such should be varied to suit your interests. A failure to do so in normal circumstances exposes you to serious risk of loss.

Ideally, you require that you receive payment for your goods without the option of the buyer having a final say on whether payment should be made in full and when he should pay it. To avoid buyer's discretion you will require that the letter of credit is irrevocable in some way – when due, and providing you produce the agreed documentation (proof that the goods have been sent or that they have arrived at the buyer's premises), there is no way for the bank to refuse payment.

This should lead you to require that the irrevocable letter of credit is confirmed and payable by a sound bank (that is, one that can be trusted) preferably in your own country. If you agree to conditional payments in any way (and you may have to do so, depending on who needs the business the most – though remember nobody needs business that bad that they are prepared to do it for nothing) you might find that your interpretation of what should trigger off a payment does not conform to your opposite number's perception of the situation.

He can save himself some cash by holding on to money for as long as possible, and if he has a cash flow problem anyway he is more than likely to seek ways of taking credit off as many suppliers as possible, and any discretion allowed in the letter of credit might prove to be too tempting for him not to exercise it on one spurious ground or another.

The confirmed, irrevocable letter of credit with the most stringent of payment conditions protects you. What about him? If he is in a position to require some commitment from you (and this is most likely to be the case as you have competitors in world markets) he will require you to agree to a performance bond of some kind.

Briefly, a performance bond requires you to pay to him a sum of money (usually a percentage of the value of the order in the letter of credit) if you breach some condition of delivery (timing, quality, quantity etc.). Unconditional performance bonds have become increasingly popular recently. Under these your bank must pay to his bank a pre-determined sum of money if the importer merely requests it. You have no defence in this last case.

Now if you have agreed to an unconditional performance bond and he invokes it you are going to get less for your goods than you priced them at and therefore you must ensure in your negotiations that your unconditional performance bond is unstoppable if, and only if, his letter of credit meets your terms of business (that is, it is confirmed, irrevocable and paid through a sound bank). This does not remove the risk, it only minimizes the loss but, once again, a loss is better than a total loss.

Having taken all possible precautions to make sure that you are paid you might still have problems in collecting some accounts. Credit control is an important subject in business management and many a road to ruin of normally sound companies has begun by neglecting to run a sound credit control operation. I worked for six months once in a credit control department of a large expanding business (which long after I had left went bust!). Negotiating skills are required in such an operation and it ought not to be left to casual labour to run it.

Three kinds of crooks

You may have to face the task of going out to visit a client to get your money (or as much of it as you can manage under the circumstances). This requires a lot of guts and determination. Debt collecting has never been one of civilization's most popular professions. Many people regard debt collectors as bullies in search of money.

In international business you cannot afford to be blasé about your debtors. Many countries, some with impeccable legal systems, can hide rogues and crooks in amongst some traders who are genuinely in temporary trouble. Few countries in the Third World would qualify as having an impeccable legal system, and some that do (for example, India) have long since had their system so clogged up with bureaucracy and place-seeking that justice has become a rare commodity and never a swift one.

177

Treating all debtors the same, irrespective of their individual and personal integrities, will tarnish your reputation (and may not get you your money). You have to visit the country and meet with the debtor to make your own judgements about the true reason for non-payment of your invoices.

There are three types of crooked dealers: those who never intended to pay in the first place and who gave every sign of not doing so but you thought you were smart enough to beat them to the honey pot (in other words, you got greedy and took risks); those who intended to pay at first but got to like the idea of not paying as they got greedy (or, you got lazy and took risks); and those who never intended to pay at all but assured you convincingly that they did (or, you got soft and took risks).

Fortunately there is an antidote to these mistakes: it's called *experience* and as you gain it you will know how to recognize the three types of crooked dealers who ultimately don't pay from those traders who do. Unfortunately, it's almost impossible in advance to separate out the non-payers from the payers, so you will only know the difference after you get paid, or not, as the case may be! Therefore, you should assume that you are dealing with a non-payer until the cash appears in your account (or bag if you have to go to collect it in person!).

For all kinds of reasons you may have accepted an order for your products that is not covered by a letter of credit of any kind, or if it is, some technical problem emerges not covered by what you thought was an irrevocable letter of credit.

The buyer agreed to pay you in due course, and he may have had every intention of so doing until 'something' came up. You will have to decide whether to wait in the hope of getting your money, or to take what you can in final settlement, or, simply, in *ultimo extremis*, to write it off as a bad debt.

Do not underestimate the need for deciding upon the latter course: far too many people can get emotionally attached to a debt problem and put time and resources into trying to collect a sum of money which are way beyond the economic gain from so doing ('it's not the amount, it's the principle' – to which the appropriate caution is: 'sometimes it is necessary to rise above principle!' and put your bad debt down to experience).

Some payment is better than none

Again, in debt situations, the broad principle applies that 'some payment is better than no payment'. Getting them to agree to some payment could take some imaginative and creative thinking on your part, followed by some carefully controlled negotiating.

Here, the thing to remember is to concentrate on your proposed remedy and not on your grievance (that they have not paid). Harping on about their failures to comply with the contract could irritate them to the point that they cease to concern themselves with your problems.

Threatening them with legal action, berating them for alleged failings, attacking their integrity and publicly humiliating them in front of their peers, are all routes to a useless deadlock. It is very easy for people to become non-available, and trying to find somebody in another country who does not want you to find them is more than you, perhaps, have time for. Get them to discuss with you your reasonable remedy for the problem and you will get closer to a solution in a shorter period of time than by any other method.

What kinds of things could you propose? Only the limits of your imagination will exhaust the possibilities. You will not only be called upon to negotiate a settlement but also, more than likely, will have to supervise its implementation.

If they can't pay you for your machinery, how about paying you in kind with some of the output from the machines? If they cannot pay you for raw materials, how about paying you with some of the worked up output? If they cannot pay you in hard currency, how about paying you in local currency to enable you to export some physical goods to sell elsewhere?

If they cannot pay 100 per cent of the debt, how about a cash payment now for 65 per cent in final settlement? If the firm to which you sent materials has gone bust before paying for the goods, how about them releasing your materials for removal from their premises in consideration of you dropping all claims on them? (If the owners won't or can't agree to this, how about – though, it's risky and probably not legal – a small 'commission' to the gatekeeper to let your lorries in over his lunch break?)

Collecting debts is a difficult and tiring job. It can also be dangerous (remember: most people love their enemies more than debt collectors). I once accompanied a collector on a visit to one of the poorer Arab countries and, after much negotiation and hassle, the Arab businessman agreed to make a settlement of £25,000 cash against a paper debt of £70,000. The problem was that the negotiation was so full of menace that we were worried about getting to the airport safely without being robbed or even worse.

When we arrived later that afternoon to collect the cash we told the importer we had just enough time to get to our hotel and collect our things before going out to the airport for the next flight home. The money was duly counted out slowly into a bag and we signed the receipt and the agreement that this was a final settlement. We had asked his people to arrange a taxi to take us to our hotel. It duly arrived and we drove off in it towards our hotel.

Two blocks along we ordered the taxi to turn off the road and reverse direction towards the border, about ninety miles away, skipping the visit to our hotel and abandoning our possessions there (which were not much in value and were visible in the form of almost empty bags waiting for us at the front desk). We showed the driver a fist full of dollars and told him if he made it to the border without stopping we would pay him a handsome fee.

This he did (and Arab drivers without doubt are the most hair-raising speed merchants in the world; at times I was not sure whether we would have been safer facing our would-be attackers). When we got to the border (about the time our plane was leaving for London) we paid the driver $100 in small bills, passed through customs, thankfully without a hitch, and caught another taxi on the other side to that country's airport.

I have no idea whether our fears were justified but relax in the knowledge that, being still alive, I have the luxury of speculating about it.

Fortunately, most of your business deals will be less dramatic and you should, on the whole, manage to complete the transaction without being menaced by wars and revolution and with payment in full for your trouble. But things do go wrong and one sure cause of them doing so is if you agree to sign something that you know in the cold light of day is not kosher. If you wish to avoid getting trapped into bad debt situations, do not sign anything that can be to your disadvantage. No business is worth the ultimate hassle of risking your future, and that of your company, in pursuit of a marginal gain. If you need business so bad that you will take unusual, extraordinary and large risks, then perhaps you ought not to be in that business at all.

Answers to self-assessment test 10

1   *(a)*   He could think you were impugning his character and this could get you into more trouble (of the 'more than it's worth' kind)   (-10)

    (b)   You are impugning his character and you are now in deep trouble (his four colleagues lounging about by his jeep are itching to show you damn foreigners who's in charge of Ogoland now!).   (-15)

    (c)   Very good, you may now drive off unmolested – though you may not get your 50 quonks change.   (10)

2   *(a)*   A good try and if your client is genuine he should agree to something like this.   (10)

    (b)   Your caution is commendable, though it might be unrealistic. Insist on something like *(a)* if you are to sign.   (5)

    (c)   Always a bad move to agree to high risk ventures which you cannot afford to lose on. If he calls up your performance bond it will cost you £23,000 no matter whether you have performed well or not. A sure road to ruin.   (-10)

3   *(a)*   Hard headed approach. It might not get you your money. Something is always better than nothing in the debt business.   (0)

    (b)   Poor response and it puts your company's £100,000 at the mercy of the Indian legal system.   (-10)

    (c)   The best move initially. See for yourself and make a judgement (that's what being a manager is all about). If his story is true you could go on to try *(d)*; if not you go to *(a)*, with the threat of *(b)*.   (10)

    (d)   A step in right direction, best after *(c)*.   (5)

Self-assessment test 11

1 You are in highly competitive negotiations with an Indonesian government agency and you suspect your rivals are desperate to get the business. You are approached one evening at your hotel by somebody who offers to sell you a copy of your rival's quotation. Do you:
   (a) Ask 'how much?'
   (b) Say 'no'?
   (c) Call the police?

2 While you are negotiating a deal to develop an oil field, you are handed a file by your opposite number that contains the printouts of the well test borings done in the area by the exploration company. On taking these back to your hotel you find inside the file an unsealed envelope marked confidential and titled clearly as a detailed proposal to develop the wells from your competitor whom you know is in the running for the contract. Do you:
   (a) Open the envelope to read and copy the details?
   (b) Keep the envelope closed?

3 Sanctions have been imposed on Ogoland by the United Nations but, by dint of your highly specialized knowledge, you know of a way to supply Ogoland with consumer goods with small risk of detection and with a certainty of high profits. Do you:
   (a) Approach the Ogoland government with details of your scheme and a cash contract to implement it?
   (b) Decline to do so and instead approach your own government with a view to having the gap plugged that you have spotted?
   (c) Approach somebody else whom you know is sympathetic to Ogoland and offer to sell the scheme to him?

12 Negotiating close to the wire
or, how politics inhibit trading

The end of free trade

That free trade would be beneficial to all is one of those undoubted truths that have been central to economic theory since Adam Smith. As Rousseau might have put it: trade is better free but everywhere it is in chains. How can this be? Largely because those who would fetter trade in some way do so because they can gain more at somebody else's expense.

The problem with governments (recognized long ago by Adam Smith) is that they listen to plausible but nevertheless nonsensical demands for protection for their constituents, which are always dressed up as sacred expressions of the 'national interest', when in fact they are merely the special pleading of people who want to make a cosy living at the consumers' expense.

Smith himself was pessimistic about the chances of the British government in the 1770s following his advice by liberating trade, and it took more than sixty years before his advice was applied. Meanwhile, free trade principles never really caught on anywhere else and by the early twentieth century the world had swallowed one protectionist policy after another. When Britain finally succumbed to protectionism in the 1930s the scene was set for the worst depression the capitalist world had seen, made far worse by the 'export unemployment' policies of the world's major trading partners.

At the end of Hitler's war the major trading partners saw sense for a while and embarked on an ambitious programme of eliminating tariff and non-tariff barriers. While these momentous negotiations were underway they adopted a temporary measure known as the General Agreement on Tariffs and Trade (GATT).

Unfortunately, the special pleading of the far from undefeated proponents of protection within the countries resulted in a very cautious approach to major reforms of world trade rules and the 'temporary' GATT provisions became permanent. This has meant a forty-year slow march through gradual reductions in tariffs (the so-called Dillon, Kennedy and Tokyo rounds of negotiations) rather than a sudden bonfire of all the restrictions that exist in world trade.

The world is poorer as a result, or rather, it is less rich than it could have been. Countries still have protected industries which both force up the price that consumers pay for the goods producers insist on making within their own borders, and oblige taxpayers to heavily subsidize these sunset industries. Meanwhile, lower cost, often better quality goods of the same type are available from foreign sources but are kept out by quotas and other restrictions or priced out by penal tariffs.

The delay in abandoning protection in all countries has led to renewed efforts to re-institute even stiffer protection to cope with the problems brought about by the current world recession. Fortunately, this drive to rebuild the ruinous protectionism of the 1930s depression has been held back – though not entirely defeated – by memories of that previous experience which undoubtedly worsened and prolonged the Great Depression.

How long this flimsy barrier to protectionism will continue depends on how long the current depression continues, and we must be pessimistic when we note the rousing chorus of protectionism articulated by political candidates and parties recently.

Thus, those of you who embark on a career of exporting your company's products, in competition with other foreign companies and those that are located within the importing country, must face up to the fact that free trade is not a fact of business life and that governments in overseas countries at least replicate the restrictive trade practices of your own country and probably add in a few other obstructions as well.

Government restrictions

We do not have space to go into a comprehensive discussion of all the restrictions imposed on trade by governments throughout the world, and anyway that is not my purpose in raising the issue. What I want to convey to you is a feel for the restrictive environment in which your exporting and importing activities will have to operate.

Governments are sovereign powers within their territories and jealously guard their authority. As a foreigner you have limited rights and one of them does not include the privilege of ignoring the regulations laid down by the government of the territory that you wish to trade in.

There are several ways in which you can do business with the people of another country.

You can export your goods direct to the country using whatever transport is convenient. Some countries might require you to use their national shipping or airlines, and not go into the free market looking for the best deal.

When your goods get to the borders of the country concerned they will have to have appropriate documentation correctly filled in and duly stamped with approvals, often from more than one source within the government's apparatus, and they might have to fulfil various restrictive criteria (quotas, quality, non-infestation, no inputs from some embargoed third parties – the Arab boycott of Israel, for example).

They may have to wait at the entry port while they are 'inspected' by government officials (or have to be taken at your expense to some obscure place for the same – the French did this with Japanese video recorders for a while, in retaliation for the often prolonged 'inspections' required by Japanese law before imports can be distributed in Japan).

Once released, you should be able to distribute them in the country for sale, but other restrictions may apply here. For instance, you may not be permitted (or might not be able to do so because the entire distribution network is a closed business for foreigners, as it is in Japan and effectively is in Scandinavia, particularly in Finland) to sell the goods directly to consumers and might have to enter into some form of agency agreement with a national company.

Agency agreements are required in most Arab countries, and many others require at least partnership status for their nationals. Brazil has heavy restrictions on direct imports through a licensing arrangement and this effectively forces would-be exporters to Brazil into partnership in joint ventures with local firms.

You will have to find a suitable local national or company with which to do business before you send off the first consignment. This can be a hit and miss affair. Not every business in the world is automatically compatible with others and, though the contacts you make might first appear to be with people of sound mind, bank balance and body, events could demonstrate your fallibility in picking 'winners'. Getting out of a joint venture that you ventured into as an adventure could prove to be more difficult than you expected.

When you are dealing in projects worth many millions of dollars, you need not just be dealing with a local company. The government of the territory could very well be in charge of the proposal, if not the negotiations, and this adds a round of complications to the purely business aspects of the deal. Governments are run by politicians and politicians face numerous pressures, some of them totally antithetical to the interests of commerce and trade. The civil servants whom you negotiate with could be under instructions from their political masters to introduce into the deal terms and conditions wholly unnecessary to its commercial success, and, perhaps worse, directly contrary to profitability.

Where governments have set up procedures to process business proposals between foreigners and nationals you can bet your next pint of chianti that these procedures take time to go through, if only because of the heavy demands upon the personnel operating them on an increasing number of would-be traders. This, of course, opens up opportunities for 'greased' queue jumping, which serves to prolong the procedures even more for those without the 'grease'.

Goods in – money out

All of the above arrangements only get your goods (perhaps) to the country itself. You still have to get your money out and here an entire battery of exchange control regulations awaits you like an obstacle course for determined commandos. The remittance of profits is always contentious and it's no different with the remittance of income.

Getting paid is not determined by the normal rules of business – somebody who buys your products must pay for them – for it depends greatly on the economic policies and circumstances of the country with whom you would trade. You can check the payment status of a country with your own government agencies or the international division of your bank.

Given that getting paid by your own government can take time, you ought not to expect too much in the way of haste from a foreign government. The slowness of the British government to pay its bills is notorious among British contractors – it's the largest single complaint in surveys – and many overseas Commonwealth governments have adopted British administrative systems for

IF IT'S FOOD, STALL IT

A Third World country was in dire need of emergency food supplies and a Western country decided to ship out its spare grain to help feed the famine area.

It contracted a shipping line who quoted $5 a ton to ship the food out to the country, a journey requiring about three weeks in all because of the distance between the ports.

When the ships arrived off the coast they had to off-load into lighters to get the food into the warehouses on shore. The local lighter owners charged $5 a ton to ship the grain over a distance of 450 yards to the warehouses.

On the next trip, four weeks later, the company's ships had to wait to off-load because the warehouses were still full of the grain from the previous trip. The grain had not been moved inland to the famine areas because of delays at customs in clearing the grain for import. This was of no direct concern to the shipping company as they were paid demurrage for every ton they delivered that stayed within the port area.

Nevertheless, the shipping managers thought the whole episode reflected badly on the governments involved in the deal. Old hands thought this was typical of the famine business which in their view (perhaps more than a trifle cynical) was only an excuse for the politicians to feel good about fixing a relief operation, with attendant publicity, without anybody following up the actual deliveries to those who badly needed them. The local customs guys were only doing their jobs and were not concerned with the wider issues of why the excess grain imports were needed in the first place – nobody from central government apparently informed them.

running their affairs. If these delays are likely to cripple you – and they can last for a year or more – you had better review your need to do business with them.

Thus, government restrictions and interventions in trade between their nationals and you are of considerable significance and you must take a realistic look at them before embarking on a trading venture abroad. In one sense this is the purpose behind some of the restrictions – to deter trade – and the purpose behind the rest of the restrictions is to control trade. Both purposes are served by the mountains of paper that govern trade between countries and you must be familiar with them if you wish to survive commercially.

Political restrictions

If the normal restrictions, discussed above, were all that you had to worry about, that would be bad enough, but there is another layer of restrictions imposed on world trade that has a more political purpose behind it than simply deterring or controlling trade for economic reasons. I refer to the various sanctions and embargoes that operate around the world.

For example, the sixteen members of the North Atlantic Treaty Organisation operate a trade embargo on the export of certain goods to countries of the Soviet bloc through the Co-ordinating Committee on Export Controls (COCOM). This economic embargo is aimed at preventing war materials, or materials that could be used in a military role, from being exported from the technologically advanced Western countries to what is regarded as a potential enemy alliance (the Warsaw Pact or WARPAC).

Items on the COCOM lists cover the obvious ones of munitions and military equipment, atomic energy materials and plants, plus a long list of items under an 'industrial and commercial' category. It is this last list that creates the most controversy between companies in the West and their respective governments (who administer COCOM regulations). To remove an item on any of the lists (and there are about 150 items on the industrial and commercial list) requires the unanimous consent of all the NATO members, in principle, but as each government is responsible for the interpretation of whether an item qualifies for the list or not, there is a side-controversy always going on as one government approves an item while another does not.

All your trade with Eastern bloc countries, including China, will require to meet the COCOM regulations, which adds yet another round of complications to your negotiations with the authorities in these countries (discussed in Chapters 4 and 8), so you had better make sure you are only committed to the deal if you get export clearance from your own government and COCOM.

Another level of politically motivated trade restrictions concerns the sanctions and embargoes on specific countries. The Arab states, for example, embargo any company trading with them from also trading with Israel. They include a clause in their contracts requiring you to agree that you support the Arab boycott of Israel and if you do not sign this clause you do not get the business, unless you are big enough, like the United States government, to refuse – the Saudis want US military equipment more than they want their signatures in support of the boycott!

How you handle this demand is a policy problem, not a negotiating issue. Of course, the imposition of the clause in practice may be less searching than the clause suggests. But as I have said they do not admit you to their countries if your passport has an Israeli visa or evidence that you have visited or are about to visit Israel in it. You must carry two passports in this case. Open flouting of the boycott could be enough to have you black-listed, but covert and unpublicized trade with Israel might be tolerated (unless it is in military equipment or in materials destined for the occupied territories).

You need not take any political boycott as absolute. There is evidence, typically of a kind that is difficult to prove, that even Arab states will trade with Israel under certain circumstances. (There is an old Israeli joke about the enmity between the Arabs and the Jews which has one Israeli asking another why the Arabs insist on having so little to do with them: 'Why do they insist on paying retail when they could get it wholesale?')

There is always constant pressure to impose sanctions on South Africa. These already exist in respect of military equipment, especially equipment that can be used internally. But the fact is that South Africa's neighbours, out of sheer economic necessity, do trade with her in a whole range of commodities and would themselves be severely damaged if sanctions were imposed on them by the rest of the world.

Economic sanctions have a very poor record of political success, though this does not stop them being imposed from time to time. If your business happens to be caught in the middle of a sanctions war you need not necessarily write off your business.

Sanctions were imposed on Italy before Hitler's war for its invasion of Ethiopia. The Soviet Union promptly stepped in and supplied Italy with the oil that was being withheld by member states of the League of Nations.

The sanctions imposed on Rhodesia (now Zimbabwe) during 'UDI' were notorious for their ineffectiveness. If anything, the range and availability of imported goods in Rhodesia during the height of the sanctions were greater than they now are in Zimbabwe after the war has ended. South Africa refused to apply sanctions against her northern neighbour – for political reasons – and most companies within the member states of the United Nations arranged their affairs so that their South African subsidiaries diverted goods northwards.

The classic case was the oil embargo on Rhodesia through the Beira pipeline (which Lonrho owned and had to close down). Independent tankers simply supplied Rhodesia through other ports in Mozambique and South Africa.

Sanction busting

Sanction busting is a lucrative business and it is likely to undermine any politically motivated interference in trade – apart from the prospects of other governments refusing to go along with the sanctions war, such as the Soviet Union and South Africa.

When a country is under sanctions pressure, it is open to proposals to supply it with what it needs. It is also generally willing to pay an over-the-odds premium for those supplies and this alone is sufficient to attract maverick and cowboy operators to move in. Whenever a country is in trouble of this kind, especially during a war, its downtown hotels are full of opportunists offering deals to government officials to supply this or that on a grand scale.

During the Falklands war, the world was scoured by, or on behalf of, the Argentinians for military supplies and some items reportedly were secured from French, South African and Israeli sources.

The same has been happening in Iran over the past two years. Tehran has had its share of traders offering deals in military spares for its army and airforce, and, reportedly, the Israelis, through third and fourth parties, have been lending a judicious hand in some deals, on the principle that the enemy of my enemy (Iraq) is worthy of some little support.

Should you go in for this business? Not if you are of a nervous disposition. When the world sees a honey pot, the place near it gets crowded and not all of those offering deals and mega-deals are in any position to deliver anything like what they promise. This imposes on the government's negotiators an onerous task of sorting out the 'wallies' from the rest.

Chancers, opportunists, merchants of fantasies, time-wasters, deluded crooks, conmen and enemy agents form a flood outside the doors of government officials with money to burn and not a lot of

'ONLY FIVE MINUTES MORE CLUB'

During the 1970s, international business negotiators regaled each other with tales (some of which must have been sheer fantasy) of the 'five mile high club'. Apparently, you joined this informal club if you participated in sexual relations while flying at over 30,000 feet (obviously in a 747 or a DC 10 – surely only these aircraft have room for such shenanigans?).

I always thought that such a 'club' must have been fairly exclusive and I was discussing the same with an American in a bar in Georgetown, Washington DC, when he told me about another, even more exclusive club, but this was one that I was not in a hurry to join.

He said he was a founder member of the 'only five minutes more club'. I asked him to explain.

'Well, it's like this', he said. 'I was in the last plane out of Phnom Penh, Cambodia, and only five minutes more on the runway and we would have been learning Vietnamese.'

I asked him what he was doing there and he said, without the slightest blush or apology: 'trying to lift out three Cambodian families for half a million dollars in diamonds. Unfortunately, I had to leave the diamonds on the tarmac and two of the families. I regret the diamonds because that was my means of paying off the pilot – he nearly crashed the plane when he heard what I had left behind but, between his anger and the Vietnamese, I think I was right to get the hell out of there at the precise moment when I did, even if I had to leave a fortune behind in doing so.'

The nearest I have got to the 'only five minutes more club' was to catch the fifth last plane out of Beirut during one of their outbreaks of civil violence and I can say in all honesty that is the closest I ever want to be to qualifying for membership. In the meantime I'm still looking around to qualify for the much safer five mile high club!

time to get what they need. In the rush to sort things out, the officials can take arbitrary actions against individuals in order to discourage all but the most genuine and serious suppliers.

The salutary example of somebody they believe is a time-wasting conman being badly maimed, or worse, has the effect of emptying the corridors as fast as they filled up. If you are a serious trader and have the resources to organize an operation on this scale, and can take the strain of running what is often a strictly illegal and certainly an embarrassing activity if your government finds out about it, you could make a financial killing.

If you are not troubled by your conscience, you have no reason not to engage in this business. Indeed, your government may be neutral in respect of the political issues at stake and, while not giving you any blessing, they may not try to do anything to stop you either (for example, the weekly flights from Stansted to Uganda during Amin's reign of terror were not illegal in Britain but were not approved).

But the same rules of trade still apply, only more so: get paid in cash close to delivery, and up-front if possible, and keep your promises even if the side you are supporting is losing.

I know a guy who forgot the last part and thought he had got away with it when the government was overthrown, only to find he was being pursued by the former government officials, now exiles, who wanted 'their' money back and were prepared to kill him if they couldn't get it. Sensible man, he gave it back and went off to look for some other less risky way to get rich.

(A politician, now dead, was a 'treasurer' for a revolutionary movement in the Third World which eventually came to power. He died, and the money – several tens of thousands of pounds in foreign currency – apparently 'disappeared'. The government concerned has still not given up finding it or punishing the persons responsible – in fact one man they caught up with was shot in Madrid some years back.)

So if you fly out to Ogoland with a brilliant scheme to help a beleaguered government get the things it needs badly, you know the risks and rewards and you ought to ensure that they are reflected in your opening negotiating position, which, if the circumstances are desperate enough, might be closer to where you get a settlement than you would otherwise expect it to be.

Dirty tricks
Competition selects winners and in doing so also selects the losers. Not everybody approaches losing with the same philosophical acceptance as you or I do, and we must therefore be aware of the

pressures on those who don't like losing to try to do something to improve their chances.

The world of business is populated with people, and people in business are like people in most other lines of life: they are susceptible to gossip, rumour, innuendo and outright deceit. This gives rivals a potential life-line if they are feeling pessimistic about their chances of getting the deal. They can blacken you in the eyes of your potential clients.

The use of dirty tricks in the search for business is legendary across the whole world. It is not confined to people in dirty macs selling dubious postcards and video nasties. Complaints about the use of dirty tricks have emanated from some of the most prestigious of board rooms, though naturally what constitutes a dirty trick depends very much on the perception of the 'victim'.

You will hear negotiators complain that their rivals cut their prices to get the business, which seems to me to be unfortunate more than unfair. Some time ago, when a British shipyard lost an order to a Finnish yard, it complained that, on its calculations, the Finns could not even pay for the materials for the ship for the price they were quoting and therefore the government must be subsidizing the deal. The Finns replied that they were not subsidizing anything and challenged the British to prove it. The row went on for a while, but the feeling that there was something underhand going on persisted, though no evidence was forthcoming to establish this.

Pre-emptive 'underhand' moves are likely to be justified on the grounds that if they are not undertaken the result will be that the business goes to a rival who, anyway, is suspected of being willing to sink to underhand moves!

I am not going to discuss the lunacy of price-cutting as a way of securing business as I have fully dealt with that elsewhere (including in *Everything is Negotiable!*) and I do not think that such methods, in the dirty tricks sense, are really underhand, only stupid. Dirty tricks are comprised of two major techniques: blackening, or bad-mouthing, you and your company to potential or current clients (which stops you getting or keeping the business); and unauthorized access to information about your negotiating position or business operation (which enables a rival to pitch their deal in a more attractive and devastatingly competitive way).

In foreign trade you are doubly exposed to dirty tricks, if only because of the distances between you and your customers. In your absence, your rivals can be in contact with your client's personnel and, by dint of charm, plausibility and outright lying, inculcate a picture of you and your operation that is at variance with the facts. It is common in business to find individuals in any company more disposed to one supplier than to another – each supplier has its supporters and detractors in a client organization and, like anybody else where something is at stake, you have to pay attention to your constituency.

It does not take much to knock you out of the running and, if you neglect your supporters (fail to visit the country enough times to be on hand to support them supporting you, or visibly let the client down in some way with deliveries, quality or spares), your rivals will use these incidents in the constant propaganda war against you.

A single failure could let them in the door on a 'trial' basis and you could be out of the door for good, or at least have to share the business with somebody else. Hence, visit your clients regularly and maintain contact with them in-between through letters, telexes and telephones. Get your people to back up your hard won negotiated deal with an all-levels approach to communicating with all levels in the client's organization. Thus, when your rivals turn up and try to set hares running against you, the initial defences of good, because they are regular, personal relations between your people and the client's should see them off. At the very least you will get an early warning of any moves in this area by rivals because you can be sure that their people will tell yours about what was said.

How about the dirty trick of industrial and commercial espionage? Here again you have a problem when you are negotiating abroad. You are a long way from home and you are forced to use insecure communications to refer matters back or to get some guidance on a new issue.

Look at the issue of security. The clerk in the postal department may have been bought by the opposition to open and copy your correspondence, complete with price quotes and specifications. Nor can you be sure that your client's filing cabinets are immune to similar intrusions. There is not a lot that you can do about this (though you can refrain from using your client's post room to send messages home – use the post office instead).

Your own communications to your home base and the security arrangements there are within your control, up to a point. Those companies that engage in proper security procedures for sensitive commercial information are better placed to ensure some immunity from dirty tricks than those that are completely lax.

If what you have is worth stealing then somebody somewhere might endeavour to steal it. So you should take simple precautions to keep your valuables (in this case information) to yourself.

Negotiators who have to report everything back while abroad are more vulnerable to having their information intercepted (listening in on an extension, bugging the hotel telephone, copying your telex messages, photocopying your price lists and conditions and other papers left in 'safe' places etc.). It is better to give long distance negotiators as much authority to settle as possible and allow them to minimize home calls for guidance.

For convenience, negotiators often carry with them vast amounts of information, only a proportion of which is needed for a particular negotiation. For example, a company price list and procedures manual will contain materials relevant both to domestic and international business, and yet only one or two pages of this may be relevant to the particular deal being negotiated. If this is accessed by an unauthorized person, then the information damage to you is extended way beyond the specific negotiations that you are in the country for. A simply stripping out of all unnecessary material from your file before you leave will minimize this damage (it will also give you less to carry).

A similar reason justifies my caution in Chapter 3 not to take with you large amounts of office work, unconnected with the negotiations in hand, with the intention (rarely realized) of doing some of it while travelling – not only is it additional weight to carry but it is vulnerable to a lapse in security.

In sum, you should support your overseas negotiation on a 'need to know' basis and select on a 'need to go' basis the materials that are to accompany the negotiator. The negotiator should be made responsible for the security of the company's commercial information and should be required to demonstrate the measures taken to protect that information while he or she is abroad.

What happens if you come across commercially sensitive information regarding a rival? That would depend on how you came across it. If you have stolen it or engaged in some illegal acquisition of it, you are obviously in breach of the law, and risk criminal charges. If, however, you come across it fortuitously (your rivals should be more careful with their secrets), I can see no reason why you should not use that information, if only by sending it to your home base.

A negotiator I know was engaged in detailed discussions with an overseas client. He returned to his hotel and unpacked his briefcase to work on his figures and found a set of papers included in some material given to him by the client which were his rival's quotation. He dithered for some time about this and decided to hand them back the next morning (having not dithered over reading them!). This he did, to the obvious embarrassment of his client. He did not get the business and has long wondered whether the client disbelieved his story that he acquired the papers accidentally and decided not to do business with a 'spy'.

Many negotiators acquire a facility for reading upside down the papers in front of their opposite number! Many negotiators do pencil in their negotiating positions, especially figures, and these can be seen across a table. It is, of course, a silly thing to do – to pencil in your price limits like that – and the remedy is in your hands. Also, if you leave the room with your sensitive papers on the desk, you must expect your opposite number to lean forward and read them – and he must assume that this is what you intended him to do.

Answers to self-assessment test 11

1 *(a)* I suppose you could claim that you were only trying to find out the price of the goods, and still claim impeccable integrity, though I suspect that you are fairly determined to let nothing stand in your way. You should go far in the rough and tumble business.

(10)

   (b) Surely you are someone of impeccable integrity who does not fear to lose. May you never go hungry and may all your deals be profitable.   (10)

   (c) A trifle harsh, don't you think, to shop a guy who is not harming you (unless he gets your papers!). If you feel that way, why not stick to *(b)*, otherwise I might think you are a trifle self-righteous too.   (10)
   (All these answers score the same because there is no way to rank the ethical positions of others.)

196

2 *(a)* It's probably what most of us would do. If one acquires something by accident I see no ethical reason for not reading it, though I am not so sure about copying it! (10)

(b) You may feel good about this self-denying ordnance but I suspect that nobody would believe you didn't open it, and you gain nothing from not doing so. (3)

3 *(a)* Why not? I suppose it depends on how you feel about the reasons for the sanctions (and the UN can be more than a little hypocritical in what it condemns and condones). You had better be sure that you have a serious scheme and do not waste the time of Ogoland officials as they might make an example of you. (10)

(b) Only the most pressing of humanitarian reasons would incline me to follow this line. The fact that you are prepared to do so without knowing why the sanctions have been imposed indicates a less than free trade attitude to business. Perhaps you are a career civil servant? (-10)

(c) Nice one. It manages to meet one's own ideas about ethics and also make a profit out of somebody else's. It could get you awarded the Gold Star of Ogoland with Oak Leave Clusters as well as a couple of thousand quid. (10)

13 The long distance negotiator

*or, a salute to those who go out
and get the business*

What's it all about?

This final chapter is by way of a short salutation to the men and
women who go out at all times of the year and get the business that
their country depends upon. Without exports we could not pay for
our imports, and without imports we would be both poorer and at
the mercy of over-protected domestic producers who know (and
they all do!) how to take advantage of the lack of international
competition.

Undertaking business abroad is no easy task and it takes a special
breed of executive who is willing to fly off (often at too short a
notice) to a distant land and negotiate on behalf of their company,
many employees of which care little about what is being done in
their name and know even less about what is involved in doing it.

Faraway places, like green fields, can look very attractive at a
distance. Go through the hassle of getting there and of functioning
in what is, after all, for you a strange environment, and you begin to
appreciate the kind of job which keeps you close to your hearth.

This is not to say that international business negotiators are all
tired, worn out and boring. I met a fresh-faced lass only last month
who was simply oozing with enthusiasm for her new job as an
international representative for a designer clothes company. She
was on one of those round robin trips that take in a handful of
European capitals in five days (naturally I refrained from advising
her where to stay in each capital!) and she was positively keyed up to
go out and get the job done. I admired her enthusiasm though I
could not share it, as I was returning from a particularly gruelling
sixteen hour a day week with a client in Sweden.

There is no doubt that the international negotiator is one of the
great unsung heroes of modern times. As world trade increases, the
role of the international negotiator is growing commensurate with

the job in hand. Goods do not sell themselves – would that they could! – and it takes hard work in many different environments to get the business to keep the goods flowing from one country to the next.

In international business many are called and few are chosen but still hundreds and thousands of new faces join the ranks each year and try their best to extend their company's business or hold on to what it has already. Those that fall by the wayside are the necessary casualties in a continuous striving for business deals the world over; those that persevere deserve their material rewards, for they certainly do not acquire them easily.

Visit any airport
International negotiating requires travel and travel soaks up energies as sure as any sport, only the strain is prolonged over longer periods.

At any airport you will see scores of negotiators embarking or disembarking, or more likely waiting in-between flights, each carrying with them the hopes and the future of their company. What these men and women do when they get to where they are going can determine whether there is a company to come back to, or one worth making long-term plans for.

You can tell the negotiators from the tourists. Negotiators travel more often to more places and consequently they are more at home in the complex tangle of an airport. They move about with an air of certain purpose about them rather than fidget their way from the indicator board to the gates.

The smarter negotiators seldom have too much luggage with them (tourists always have too much of everything, except patience) and they are organized for their flight. If they are in company they form a merry band, swapping stories of their last deal and their hopes for the next. In this sense, they are like sales staff the world over who regale each other with tales and jokes, mutual 'atrocity' stories of this or that dealer they all know; when, that is, they are not slashing into the reputations of their colleagues in other functions who don't understand anything about how tough it is out in the field.

There is a camaraderie among international business negotiators, partly expressing their competence and their pride in their work, and partly their inner tensions about the next deal that they must tackle. True, some of them (all of them at one time or another!)

talk-up the deals they have negotiated – a little exaggeration here or there is as surely par for the course among negotiators as it is among those who would catch fish by rod and line. Mostly these little peccadilloes are harmless invasions of personal integrity and are mostly caused by the need to appear worthy of one's trade in a world where it is not always sensible to go into the details of a private commercial deal.

When you next sit in an airport lounge – for, be sure, if you travel at all by air you will sit in some lounge for some time, perhaps for longer than you planned – look around you at your fellow travellers. Having separated out the tourists, check over the others. Most of these will be travelling on business. If you count them you will be surprised just how many men and women fly out for this reason only.

You will spot the first-timer, nervously checking and re-checking his or her ticket, ever willing for someone to talk to them so they can confirm their status and appear more confident than they feel. The old-timer will probably be pretending to be totally relaxed, even dozing to prove it, though his ears will be well attuned to departure announcements through his deepest of cat naps. Their faces will show the years, in some cases better than others, but the lines will be worn with the pride of experience. So will the condition of their bags – working bags, a trifle battered but everywhere serviceable in every condition they might encounter, no smart Sunday supplement luggage sets for them!

Between the new and the retiring come the vast mass of business negotiators, in all shapes and sizes, in all temperaments and moods, waiting for the 'off' like a marine-packed landing craft on D-Day. Those who want to talk and socialize will – it is from this band that you get all the advice on where to stay and what to do about foreign exchange rip-offs – and those who want to travel in solitude and contemplation will try to do so, either by physically slinking crabwise away from the hearty souls looking for a foursome for a bridge game from London to Bahrain (or just somebody with whom to drink their duty-frees), or they will immerse themselves in a large paperback.

I know one guy in search of being left alone who prominently displays about him a couple of issues of *Watchtower*, a Jehovah's Witnesses newspaper, because nobody but nobody seeks to get into a long conversation all the way to Tokyo with somebody they think is a religious proselytizer!

200

Ten good rules for negotiating for business, anywhere
The best of the breed of international business negotiators have several things in common. Observe them at work, imitate them, improve upon what you learn, and you will join their ranks.

- **First**, you must get used to the idea of being a foreigner. There is no substitute for the acquisition of a little national humility. You don't have to go overboard the other way and renounce your birthright ('go native' it used to be called in the Empire). But you must accept your place as a foreigner in the order of things, and this means above all accepting that the world neither owes your country a living nor does it necessarily owe it a good turn. What you get from them will depend upon how much they think they need what you are offering in exchange, and if they can get a better deal elsewhere they should and will take it.

- **Second**, you must get yourself organized for international business travel. Those who want to be the most successful negotiators fly first or business class, stay in good quality hotels, take with them only that which they need, do not regard a long flight as an excuse for a boozy party and are sensible about the very real problems of jet-lag (they only go to bed in other time zones when it is time to do so there, not when they feel like it on arrival).

- **Third**, you must learn something about the manners and customs of the people with whom you want to do business. You should not assume that anything that is quite acceptable in your culture is necessarily acceptable in all other cultures. One way to improve your acceptability as an international negotiator is to learn something of the language of the people with whom you deal.

  This advice also applies to those countries where the people speak a language akin to your own. For example, Australians and most North Americans speak recognizable English, but you would be foolish to leave it at that when you go to these countries to negotiate. The English-speaking peoples are separated by their common language, and you would be well advised to gen up on the local slang, dialect, and manners if you want to do business with your 'cousins'.

  If you have any doubts on this score, think about the differences in approach within the tiny British Isles between the English and the Scots, and then consider how different the

Australians etc. have become from both English and Scots over the years of separation.

When dealing with non-English-speaking peoples the advice is the same, only more so. Japanese manners and courtesies are entirely different from those of the Mid-West of the United States. Fortunately, once you observe them, you can adjust without too much discomfort to your sense of what is right or wrong – though Japanese bathtime might be a tiny surprise the first time!

- **Fourth**, you must adjust the pace of your negotiating to that of the people with whom you are keen to do business (they might have to do the same if they visit you in your country). It is no good trying to do anything much in a hurry, and it is absolutely hopeless to expect to be able to ginger them up just because Father Time is knocking on your schedules.

  In most parts of the world you will have to slow down (in the US of A you will probably have to speed up), and it does not matter whether the delays are caused by bureaucratic procedures (the Soviet Union etc.) or by the way they make decisions (Japan and the Middle East). Have patience, take longer, and don't give yourself unrealistic schedules.

- **Fifth**, you must develop those skills of negotiating that are the same the world over. Beginning with preparation (or knowing your own business better than your rivals), you must know how to listen, react to what you hear, make conditional propositions ('If, then perhaps'), re-package creatively and bargain using conditional, and only conditional, offers ('If, then'). You can check out your performance in this vital area by reading *Managing Negotiations* and *Everything is Negotiable!*.

- **Sixth**, you must always remember that in a negotiation with anybody anywhere you always have the option of saying 'no' to a deal that is in anyway suspect, whether your suspicions concern the contract they want you to sign, the terms they want you to agree to, or the business ethics they want you to abandon.

  You do not need to sign anything that does not meet your best and long-term interests, but if you do sign something you ought not to have then you will have to live with it (or without it).

  This is all the more true when you have been working hard for a long time to get some kind of deal. You must adopt the attitude that 'bygones are bygones' and previous investment in

202

time and energy can never be recouped, and certainly you must never try to do so by agreeing to something that is not strictly what you can live with.

Hence, if Soviet negotiators want you to take goods in place of cash, or Germans want you to accept penalty clauses for delivery commitments, or Chinese negotiators want you to cut your prices on a 'sell cheap, get famous' promise, or Australians want your goods on a consignment only basis, or Americans want exclusive US of A rights, or Arabs want 15 per cent commission, or Ogolanders want side-payments in a numbered Swiss account, or whatever (and there will be many 'whatevers'!), you should always remember that, though you have the authority to say 'yes', you also have the responsibility for what you say 'yes' to. So perhaps, you should say 'no' a little more often?

- **Seventh**, you must cultivate the habit (until it requires no effort whatsoever) of never getting involved in discussions or comments upon any country's politics, religion, way of life, ethics of doing business, racial mix, legal processes, constitutional arrangements, methods of selecting their leaders, public or private morality, prevalence of tips, bribery and corruption, modes of dress or undress, laws regarding your personal preferences in sex, booze, drugs, porno videos, press freedom and citizens' rights.

If you wish to combine a business career with reforms of other countries you should reconsider your personal prospects. The internal affairs of other countries are none of your damn business and in many parts of the world they do not take kindly, or treat lightly, interfering visitors who forget what their visas say they are there for.

Your wonderful views on democracy, feminism, the free market, income distribution, social welfare, local wars, racial strife, the treatment of offenders and such-like should be left at home, and if in your case that is not possible then you should stay at home too!

- **Eighth**, you must treat everybody with whom you deal with the greatest of personal respect, no matter how you feel about the way the negotiation is being handled. This applies to personnel on your own side as well as on the other side (even if you feel some of your people seem to be working for them too!). Respect for the individual in business life is always a rare treat if you are on the receiving end of it, and, for that reason alone, it is well worth adopting as a policy for your own behaviour towards others.

No matter how new and strange to you any culture is in the world, and no matter how intricate are the social obligations of the people you deal with, you can be sure of being accepted anywhere, in spite of any courtesy gaffes you make out of your ignorance or forgetfulness, if you display constant evidence of your respect for your opposite number as a person. There are no parts or peoples of the world where you will find exceptions to this principle; everybody reacts more warmly to those whom they can see respect them than they do to those whom they suspect do not.

- **Ninth**, you must always endeavour to the best of your ability – and sometimes beyond that – to meet the terms of the contracts you negotiate and agree to. Each deal for you has to be a personal as well as a company commitment. Your role does not finish when the signatures are recorded. In many respects it continues through the lifetime of the deal.

You must take a personal interest in what happens thereafter and be ready to use your good and best offices to get things put right that manifestly are wrong. Good and enduring personal relations between negotiators will lead to long-term relationships between their companies and it is from this that the mutual prosperity of trading partners grows.

Your best action is always to follow through on a deal – call the other guy on the phone, or drop into see him on your next visit, to check that everything that you agreed to is actually happening and that he is well satisfied with the outcome. In other words, you do not sign the contract, grab the cash and run. Follow through and follow up if there are any problems. Your pride alone should incline you to do so, but your long-term best interests should make it mandatory.

- **Tenth**, in deciding how to conduct your business affairs abroad, particularly when operating in parts of the world where social licence is somewhat slacker than it is elsewhere, you must be guided by what you feel comfortable doing rather than by what you feel is right or wrong.

This is by no means a prescription for abandoning the distinction between right and wrong – quite the reverse! – nor is it a prescription for turning you into a hardened cynic. The facts of life are that many parts of the world with which your country trades do have different standards of personal conduct and these standards influence whether you get business, or even get around the country itself, and you will have to learn to live with this and adapt to it, or you will not do business there.

Deciding on what is right in the circumstances is no easy matter, and it is, therefore, a highly personal decision which you cannot pass on to somebody else. What you will be advised to do by people sitting on their safe and comfortable seats back home may be fine for an assembly of ostriches approaching a sandy beach but absolutely useless for you as you go down the ramp from your aircraft and approach the ranks of officialdom at customs and immigration (and the serried ranks of their colleagues along the corridors of the ministries you need to get past to complete your negotiations). It is you that is faced with the moral dilemmas in Ogoland and you who must decide what to do about what you face there.

It is presumptuous of me to advise you on this matter, except perhaps to suggest that you talk to the older hands about it on a country-by-country basis. Listen to what they have to say, reflect on the fact that billions of dollars worth of business is being conducted every year in that environment, and decide on a case-by-case basis what you feel most comfortable about doing (remember the sixth rule about your right to say 'no').

Negotiate abroad!

Your journey through this book is almost over and I hope that it is a prelude to many journeys that you will make in pursuit of your commercial interests. I began by asserting that negotiating principles are the same the world over but that the way the shots are played will vary from one culture to another. I have demonstrated some of the most salient differences between some of the world's cultures (though not exhaustively and not comprehensively for every major country).

The book's central theme has been that it does not matter for what stakes you are negotiating, if you are negotiating abroad you will have to adapt your style to the dominant style of the people with whom you wish to do business, particularly if they have alternatives to what you are offering (which will almost certainly be the case in the competitive world markets we have today).

If you apply yourself to the task, approach every transaction with an open mind, spend as much time as you can going over the moves, the successes and the set-backs you experience, and above all remember that you are the foreigner, then I have no doubt that you will be able to improve your international negotiating performance and join that small elite who successfully ply their wares – anywhere that their companies send them.

Lastly, if you are passing through an airport, a hotel, a car hire centre, a ferry service, a government corridor, a company dining room or whatever, and you see me sitting about with not too much to do, why not amble across, introduce yourself, and we can swap experiences over a cup or two of coffee, or, if we are both in funds and on expenses, we might stretch ourselves and our budgets to a glass or two of the local nectar!

INDEX

Bestselling Non-Fiction

- [ ] The Alexander Principle — Wilfred Barlow — £2.95
- [ ] The Complete Book of Exercises — Diagram Group — £4.95
- [ ] Everything is Negotiable — Gavin Kennedy — £2.95
- [ ] Health on Your Plate — Janet Pleshette — £2.50
- [ ] The Cheiro Book of Fate and Fortune — Cheiro — £2.95
- [ ] The Handbook of Chinese Horoscopes — Theodora Lau — £2.50
- [ ] Hollywood Babylon — Kenneth Anger — £7.95
- [ ] Hollywood Babylon II — Kenneth Anger — £7.95
- [ ] The Domesday Heritage — Ed. Elizabeth Hallam — £3.95
- [ ] Historic Railway Disasters — O. S. Nock — £2.50
- [ ] Wildlife of the Domestic Cat — Roger Tabor — £4.50
- [ ] Elvis and Me — Priscilla Presley — £2.95
- [ ] Maria Callas — Arianna Stassinopoulos — £2.50
- [ ] The Brendan Voyage — Tim Severin — £3.50

ARROW BOOKS, BOOKSERVICE BY POST, PO BOX 29, DOUGLAS, ISLE OF MAN, BRITISH ISLES

NAME ....

ADDRESS ....

....

....

Please enclose a cheque or postal order made out to Arrow Books Ltd. for the amount due and allow the following for postage and packing.

U.K. CUSTOMERS: Please allow 22p per book to a maximum of £3.00.

B.F.P.O. & EIRE: Please allow 22p per book to a maximum of £3.00.

OVERSEAS CUSTOMERS: Please allow 22p per book.

Whilst every effort is made to keep prices low it is sometimes necessary to increase cover prices at short notice. Arrow Books reserve the right to show new retail prices on covers which may differ from those previously advertised in the text or elsewhere.